EASY RULES

.,"";?,!()

PuNCtuaTioN

Kenneth E. Delp

SOUTH-WESTERN PUBLISHING CO.

Managing Editor: Karen Schneiter
Acquisitions Editor: Janie F. Schwark
Developmental Editor I: Dianne S. Rankin
Coordinating Editor: Laurie Winget
Production Editor II: Melanie A. Blair
Designer: Nicola M. Jones
Production Artist: Sophia Renieris
Marketing Manager: Carolyn Love

Copyright © 1994

by

SOUTH-WESTERN PUBLISHING CO.
Cincinnati, Ohio

All Rights Reserved

ISBN: 0-538-61500-1

Library of Congress Catalog Card Number: 91-65665

3 4 5 6 7 8 DH 99 98 97 96

Printed in the United States of America

PREFACE

Welcome to a set of practice exercises and a quick, easy way to learn to punctuate what you write. *EASY RULES: Punctuation* is a text-workbook to help you learn to place punctuation marks accurately.

This book is different than most grammar or style guides. Those that provide rules often do not have practice exercises. Those with practice exercises do not always clearly describe the rules. *EASY RULES: Punctuation,* however, corrects both of these situations by forming a foundation with three elements:

1. The text has all of the rules for each punctuation mark in one place.
2. The text has enough practice exercises carefully sequenced so that you can build one skill upon another.
3. The text has exercises which duplicate as closely as possible the examples and explanations.

EASY RULES: Punctuation is comprehensive yet concise; it is simple yet sequential.

FEATURES

EASY RULES: Punctuation has some unique features, the most notable being the Compact Summaries for each mark of punctuation. All the rules and corresponding examples are printed there. The summaries are printed as foldouts for you to use while you work on the exercises and read the explanations. Later, after you finish with the text-workbook, you can remove the summaries and put them in a notebook or on a bulletin board and use them for future reference. Put them where they will be accessible.

In each of the summaries the grammatical terms that describe the uses are in the left column, and the examples are in the right column with a matching letter. The trick is to learn the key words associated with the rules. These rules are the ones you are likely to remember and use even when you do not have the Compact Summaries close at hand. Don't worry if you find the grammar terms hard to remember—often the examples are enough to guide you.

The exercises are presented in a sequence. The most basic rule is presented and used first followed by rules and examples that are more complex. After some explanation and examples you are asked to place the punctuation mark in sentences and give rules for each of them. Then an exercise follows that includes all of the lessons learned about that mark. This sequence allows you to build confidence in what you have learned before new rules are introduced.

TO THE STUDENT

Like most educational materials you will only get out of this book what you put into it. Although this may sound trite, it is true. After you complete some honest work with the exercises, you should have a clear understanding of most punctuation usage. There will be times when you will be confused while writing. However, the exercises in this text and the Compact Summaries will give you a basis from which to work. The exercises are not intended to be tricky or deceptive. If you find a tricky situation, that is because it arises naturally out of the practice sentences. It could also arise from the confusion that comes when the punctuation is left out of the sentences on purpose for the exercises.

Putting the rule number and letter above each punctuation mark you insert in the practice exercises is important to your learning. This method will help you develop a clear understanding of the rules and gain familiarity with the Compact Summaries. After you have finished these practice exercises, the rule numbers themselves will not be important. During the practice, however, the numbers are the key that ties the practice to the comprehensive set of rules in the Compact Summaries. Putting the rule numbers and letters in the practice exercises will also help you later to look up the rules you will need when writing your own sentences. Allow this method to help you develop confidence.

TO THE INSTRUCTOR

The pretest and posttest in the teacher's manual will give you some indication of the progress that each student makes. The tests themselves are of equal difficulty and complexity.

Use the rules. Insist that the student mark the correct rule number and letter above each use. This practice eliminates haphazard use or just putting in punctuation because it "feels" right or looks good. Without the rule numbers and letters, the changes are not significant since many people will just put the punctuation marks where they want without changing how they think about them. Using the rules is an effective teaching strategy.

Kenneth Delp

CONTENTS

INTRODUCTION

Mrs. McMurphy walked around the classroom carefully watching the students at work on their compositions. The students were to write a composition on one of the topics written on the board: Your Pet Peeve, The Value of Manners, or Peer Pressure. All the pupils were challenged with paragraph organization, sentence structure, and comma placement. The students struggled like almost everyone except English teachers with where to place that little punctuation mark, the comma. Mrs. McMurphy's rule was simple, "Put a comma where you pause."

Brandon, the student in the fourth row who followed all directions faithfully, put commas wherever he paused. His paper, now decorated with the little squiggles, caught Mrs. McMurphy's attention. "No, Brandon, your commas are not placed correctly."

"But I put them where I paused like you said," he replied.

"Yes, but you paused in the wrong places," said Mrs. McMurphy. Her rule was repeated, but it still did not help Brandon know where to place his commas. What he needed was a clear set of rules and some regular practice.

Punctuation is a necessary tool for the writer. Although the words we use carry the meaning of our thoughts, the marks of punctuation we use when writing help ensure that our readers receive our intended meaning. The writer needs to master the punctuation marks as one of the tools used to communicate accurately with readers.

Often the problem is that we do not get enough practice to learn to use the punctuation marks easily. The set of exercises and rules included in *EASY RULES: Punctuation* will help. The rules are clear. The practice is simple, straightforward, and structured. As a writer you need punctuation as a tool to communicate with your reader, and you must use that set of rules which is most familiar to the reader.

Grammar books, style guides, and writing texts usually have many rules; but they often lack enough explanation or examples. The situation is worse because these source books do not always agree with one another.

What is needed is a clear set of rules, an explanation of them, and enough practice to really learn the rules and apply them consistently. *EASY RULES: Punctuation* provides all the rules in one easy-to-use book. The result of a study of several grammar books, texts from various grade levels, style guides, editorial guides, and dictionaries are reflected in the Compact Summaries. The Compact Summaries, the explanations of rules, and the exercises easily solve most questions of punctuation usage.

THE STEPS OF PUNCTUATION

Before you begin to study all the punctuation marks and start the practice exercises in the text-workbook, remember that punctuation in English writing has several steps based on a hierarchy of strength. In Figure I–1 each punctuation mark is stronger or more of a "thought break" than the one below it.

FIGURE I–1

Steps of punctuation

(weak to strong)

end marks	?, !, and .
parentheses	( )
dashes	—
colons	:
semicolons	;
commas	,

End marks—the question mark, exclamation mark, and period—are the strongest; commas are the weakest. The weakest mark is also the most frequently used. The comma also has the greatest variety of uses. In some cases conflicts arise between different comma uses, and a stronger mark of punctuation must referee or clarify the situation.

Two other familiar marks, the apostrophe and the hyphen, are usually used to show connections and uses within words. *EASY RULES: Punctuation* has a chapter on each of the marks shown in Figure I-1 plus chapters on both the apostrophe and the hyphen.

A sentence can be rewritten several different ways with each version having a slightly different emphasis or different meaning. Thus, some matters of punctuation are judgments for the writer to make. Some rules are not absolutely black or white. The writer has some flexibility. On the other hand, some rules are always followed, and the writer who does not follow them appears uninformed or careless.

Punctuation rules should be applied consistently, but the writer must still think, consider, and judge the uses of the punctuation to convey the intended meaning. No set of rules will substitute for that responsibility of the writer to the reader.

THE COMPACT SUMMARIES

The Compact Summaries are condensed and complete. You will not have to look elsewhere for rules. Each shows the grammar rule or term in the left column and a matching example of the usage of that punctuation mark in the right column. Use both columns and work back and forth.

Make the summaries useful to you. Look up the rules when you don't know them. Use the grammar terms and rules to look up the guidelines for the uses you need. You may even make an assumption about which one of the rules applies in a situation, then search for an example in a similar sentence.

PUNCTUATION RULES

In each of the chapters that follow, you will find the information in the same format. There will be objectives for the study of each rule. The rule statement that defines the specific uses under study will be followed by some examples along with an explanation for each rule. Some minor tips and additional notes will be given with the explanation.

Objectives

The learning objectives are the goals for the section of the text-workbook associated with each rule. When you have completed each section, you should be able to meet each stated objective.

Rule statement

The rule statements in the chapters come from the Compact Summaries. Each chapter deals with a different rule so that you can study the rules and subrules individually.

Examples

An example of each rule and subrule is also taken directly from the Compact Summaries. These examples help you see how to apply each rule or subrule.

Explanation

The explanation section provides notes and more detailed descriptions on each of the uses covered by the rule. The explanation also offers some tips on how to think about the uses. Be sure to have the appropriate Compact Summary folded out as you read the information. This way you can compare the explanation to the rules as you proceed.

EXERCISES

In addition to a clear set of rules, *EASY RULES: Punctuation* has a set of exercises with a very specific structure and sequence on the usage of each punctuation mark. The exercises begin with simple uses with simple rules. The idea is to get most of them correct before you try to apply more complex rules and rule combinations.

Each of the rules on the Compact Summary has an exercise. Then a review exercise summarizes the uses up to that point. (There is no review exercise after Rule 1 because by then you have only worked with one rule.) Each exercise builds upon previous exercises and rules concerning that punctuation mark.

The exercises are easy to use. After you study the rule, use the Compact Summary as a reference and place the punctuation in the sentences where you think the marks belong. Place the rule number and letter above the mark. Placing the rule number and letter above the mark is important because you are giving a reason for inserting each mark. The numbers are not important after you finish the exercises; however, they are very important while working through each exercise. Several sentences have the same structure. Each exercise builds upon a solid base from the exercises that came before it. In this way you learn the reasons behind the punctuation. You become more confident and can understand new situations rather than just knowing by rote or guessing. Let the rules help you.

The answers for each exercise can be found at the back of the text-workbook. These exercises work effectively in a classroom or as individual practice. If you are using them in your class, work honestly. If you are working through the book on your own, study the sentences, examples, rules, and answers carefully.

Remember the method for completing these exercises. Place the marks in the sentences where they belong and write the rule number and letter from the appropriate Compact Summary over **each** mark you insert. Although this may seem obvious for the first exercises and burdensome in the later, more complicated ones, it has a purpose. You will learn more quickly, and your knowledge will last longer if you follow this procedure while completing these exercises.

SUMMARY

When you have finished working through *EASY RULES: Punctuation,* you will punctuate sentences correctly over ninety percent of the time without looking up the rule. Naturally, if you do need to look up a rule, you will have a handy place to do so which will increase your accuracy even more.

COMMA

Chapter 1 The Frequently Misused Troublemaker

The comma is the most frequently used punctuation mark. Its closest rival is the period, yet the comma is far more flexible and versatile. The comma can separate a series of items, or it can indicate a slight pause in a sentence separating two main ideas. Some of its uses are so standard, such as between cities and states, that we barely even notice them. Commas are used to mark those small separations and connections in writing. After applying the comma rules in consistent practice, you will be able to use the commas with confidence and accuracy.

SERIES
Chapter 1   *COMMA*

LEARNING OBJECTIVES

After your study of Comma Rule 1, you will be able to:
• Insert commas correctly between items in a series.
• Label comma uses to indicate whether the series is of words, phrases, or clauses.

RULE 1: Use commas between items in a SERIES.

A. Words

B. Phrases

C. Clauses

A. Bring your notebook, pen, and textbook to class every day.

B. You can remove the cover, adjust the drive belt, and replace the cover with just one tool.

C. We cannot decide what information we will store, how we will retrieve it, or how it will be used.

Fold out the Compact Comma Summary in the back of the text-workbook so you can see it while you read the explanations and work on the exercises.

COMMA—SERIES

Most people understand the basic structure of Rule 1. The structure is simply three or more items written in a row as shown in Figure 1-1.

FIGURE 1-1   Item 1 ,   Item 2 ,   and / or   Item 3
The Series structure

A. Words

Use commas in a series of words. For example, a sentence might contain a series of nouns, verbs, or adjectives. Here is an example:

> *Sumio, Tom,* and *Jennifer* went to the ball game. (nouns in a series)

B. Phrases

Use commas in a series of phrases. These combinations of words form a unit smaller than a sentence but greater than only one word. Phrases lack either a subject or a verb.

> One prescription for healthy living is to *run a mile a day, eat a balanced diet,* and *get adequate rest.*

C. Clauses

Use commas with a series of clauses. Commas can separate a series of subordinate clauses or a series of independent clauses.
Consider this example:

> The project will be complete *when we finish the paperwork, when we pay all the bills,* and *when we clean the rented building.*

A sentence must have a subject and predicate (verb) and make a complete thought. Notice that the three italicized items have subjects and predicates, but alone they do not form complete thoughts. Therefore, these items are not sentences. They are subordinate clauses.

Short sentences can also be combined into a larger sentence. These short sentences are called independent clauses.

> *You must make up your mind, you must practice daily,* and *you must believe you can succeed.*

Usually you should use a displayed list if you have more than three items.

The most controversial comma in any series is the last comma in the group—the one near *and*. Most professional writers say this comma is optional. However, they do admit that if confusion is possible, a writer should include the last comma. One easy technique to remember is to always use the comma in this situation. That way you do not have to think about it each time you want to use it. Your reader will not be confused, and you will always be consistent.

UNIQUE USES

Sometimes in a series there is a need to change a comma to a semi-colon to make the sentence clearer. Because the semicolon is a stronger mark, it may help show your meaning more clearly. See the Semicolon chapter for details on using it in a series.

The abbreviation *etc.* and the ampersand (&) are also treated differently in a series. Generally you should avoid using the abbreviation for the Latin words *et cetera* that you see as *etc.* in text. It means "and other things." If you do use *etc.* with a series, follow two rules:

- Do not use the conjunctions *and, but,* or *or* before *etc.*
- Place a comma following the period after *etc.* unless the sentence ends immediately after it.

Since the meaning of *etc.* includes "and," do not use the word again. The comma after *etc.* is unique to the situation whenever more sentence follows.

> The careful writer worries about spelling, capitalization, punctuation, margins, type style, etc., during the editing cycle.

In some company names and other uses the ampersand (&) substitutes for *and.* Avoid the ampersand in your text, but if you must use it for an official title or name, do not use a comma with the ampersand.

> We do all of our legal work with Medina, Baker & Cobble.

SUMMARY

The SERIES commas set apart the equal items in a series. The series can be made up of words, phrases, or clauses.

EXERCISE 1   RULE 1
Chapter 1   *COMMA*

- Insert commas in the following sentences and write the rule number and letter from the Compact Comma Summary above each comma you insert.
- All the uses involve only Rule 1.
- In the last five sentences one does not need commas.

Example: The teacher taught algebra,¹ᴬ biology,¹ᴬ and chemistry.

1. The tour guide was fluent in English French and German.

2. We will need excellent actors a skilled director and a willing stage crew to produce the play.

3. Lauren worked hard in her arithmetic class to understand the problem complete a solution and check her answer.

4. Your order for lumber electrical parts and roofing cannot be filled until next week.

5. You will have to take everything out sweep thoroughly and wash the floor when you clean the garage.

6. Careful reading clear class notes and thorough review can lead a student to a good test score.

7. An efficient secretary should be able to work quickly accurately and politely.

8. You must devote most of your time to the task you must take calculated risks and you must have the patience to see your plans through in order to build a financial empire.

9. We liked your suggestion the way you presented it and the cost savings it will provide.

10. Summer brought thoughts of swimming picnics and time away from school.

11. Miss Smith will not stand for any more editing mistakes feeble excuses or missed deadlines.

12. Our business plan must demonstrate a clear marketing strategy a realistic budget forecast and a plan to rent equipment.

13. The paper supply and the toner and the copier count must be checked each day.

14. We are sorry to report that your car has a transmission leak a radiator leak and two leaking shock absorbers.

15. The printer must be completely disconnected it must be taken to the shop and it must be reconditioned with new parts.

The answers are in the back of the text-workbook.

COORDINATE

Chapter 1   *COMMA*

LEARNING OBJECTIVES

After your study of Comma Rule 2, you will be able to:
- Insert commas correctly between coordinate elements.
- Label comma uses to show whether the coordinate use involves joining two clauses or separating equal modifiers.
- Insert and label commas accurately when the uses from Rules 1 and 2 are mixed in sentences.

RULE 2: Use commas in COORDINATE situations.

A. Compound sentences with a coordinating conjunction (and, but, or, for, nor, so, yet)

B. Compound sentences after a semicolon and conjunctive adverb (therefore, however, thus, ...)

C. Adjectives (only if they are reversible)

A. You must set the dial, and the ready light must be visible.

B. The storm pounded against the shutters; however, no windows were broken.

C. It is an efficient, inexpensive unit.

Fold out the Compact Comma Summary in the back of the text-workbook so you can see it while you read the explanations and work on the exercises.

COMMA—COORDINATING

The key word for this rule, *coordinate,* simply means "equal." The equal elements may be two equal sentences that combine to become a larger sentence, or the equal elements may be equal modifiers before a noun. Think of the equality like a balance as shown in Figure 1-2.

FIGURE 1-2

The coordinate structure

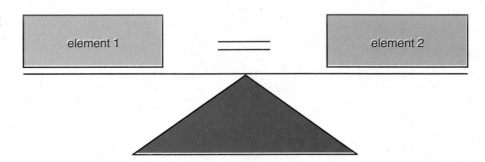

A. Compound sentences

Use a comma to separate equal, independent clauses. Sometimes you will want to join two shorter sentences to make a longer compound sentence. When each of the two sentences carry equal weight, join them with a comma and a connecting word called a conjunction. *And, but, or, for, nor, so,* and *yet* are the only words that will join sentences on an equal basis. These words are called *coordinating conjunctions.*

The words on each side of the connecting word must be complete sentences in order to use the comma. A compound sentence is like a teeter-totter balanced on the connecting word as shown in Figure 1-3. The coordinate clauses are of equal value. Each side has a subject (an "actor") and a verb (an "action").

FIGURE 1-3

Two clauses connected by a coordinating conjunction

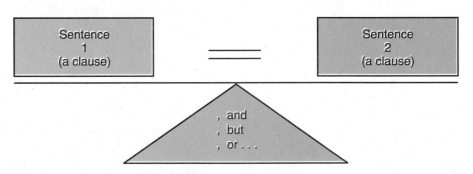

B. Conjunctive adverbs

Another way to connect two equal sentences is with a semicolon and a different class of connecting words called *conjunctive adverbs.* This term applies to the following group of familiar words:

therefore	then
however	besides
furthermore	otherwise
moreover	hence
nevertheless	anyhow

also	indeed
instead	henceforth
thus	likewise
consequently	meanwhile
accordingly	still

A comma follows the conjunctive adverb. The overall structure of this combination (see Figure 1-4) is really the same as the structure in Figure 1-3.

FIGURE 1-4

Two clauses connected
by a conjunctive adverb

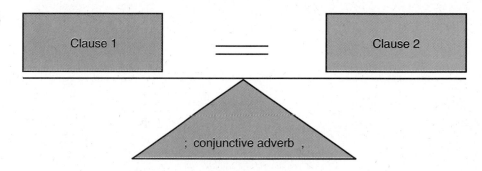

Study the following two examples. Notice that the semicolon, the conjunctive adverb, and the comma form a connecting unit.

Marcia will be the presiding officer at the meeting; however, the agenda is shorter than usual.

Charles will not complete the draft; therefore, someone else will have to finish it.

The semicolon actually joins the sentences because the connecting words (the conjunctive adverbs) are not strong enough in themselves.

Sometimes you may have to use semicolons to join compound sentences. Refer to the semicolon chapter for more detail.

C. Adjectives

This part of Rule 2 has coordinate words, equal describers called *adjectives*, instead of coordinate sentences. Not all describing situations demand commas, but these tests make it easy. If the two describing words can be reversed with no change in meaning, a comma should separate them. Another test is the "and" test. Put the word *and* between the adjectives. If the sentence still makes sense, the comma is correct, and you may leave out the word *and*.

Check these sentences using the "and" test and the reversible test.

He was a happy, agreeable person.

He was an agreeable, happy person.

He was a happy and agreeable person.

Because the "and" test works, the sentence needs a comma.

He was a happy, agreeable person.

SUMMARY

The **COORDINATE** uses of commas demand equality. Use commas with conjunctions such as *and, but,* and *or* joining two equal clauses in a compound sentence. Use commas following the semicolon and conjunctive adverbs such as *however* and *therefore*. Use commas to separate equal describers if they can be reversed or separated by *and.*

EXERCISE 2A
Chapter 1   *COMMA*

RULE 2

- Insert commas in the following sentences and write the rule number and letter from the Compact Comma Summary above each comma you insert.
- All the uses involve only Rule 2.
- In the last five sentences one does not need commas.

Example: Salary can be an important factor in a job,²ᴬ but working conditions may mean almost as much.

1. My grandfather sent us a letter at Christmas but we haven't heard from him since.

2. We can use a large hand truck or we can rent a hydraulic lift.

3. The results of our last tests indicate no immediate problem; however we should retest in six months as a double check.

4. Management finds your plan a feasible effective solution to the problem.

5. Carl designed the helpful gadget; however he does not have the business skills needed to develop an organized successful marketing campaign.

6. The upper bracket of the shelf must be fastened first and the aligning holes must be predrilled.

7. I cannot agree with your solution yet I can agree with your analysis of the problem.

8. I do not like the author's stilted arrogant style.

9. The supervisor must work skillfully with people yet she must also know the operation well.

10. Thorough research will provide the information and clear writing will make it useful to others.

11. You will have to get permission to operate the equipment or someone will be assigned to operate it for you.

12. Mr. Baker can be a reasonable man when he gets enough sleep the previous night.

13. Cathy raced to the stage to receive the award she had earned for her diligent thorough work.

14. Sam's imagination ran wild but no one paid attention when he spoke about his ideas.

15. A well-coached actor is able to deliver a confident convincing dialect.

The answers are in the back of the text-workbook.

EXERCISE 2B
Chapter 1   *COMMA*

RULES 1–2

- Insert commas in the following sentences and write the rule number and letter from the Compact Comma Summary above each comma you insert.
- All the uses involve only Rules 1 and 2.
- In the last five sentences one does not need commas.

Example: Helpful hints make taking tests easier; therefore,^{2B} learn as many of them as you can.

1. Streets bridges and railroad crossings were severely damaged during the storm.

2. Your conclusions must be based on complete data yet I do not see enough figures to justify your answer.

3. A roving eye an attentive ear and continued patience will serve the inexperienced anxious hunter well.

4. Charlie's well-developed imagination helped him as a writer but it did not solve his problems with grammar and spelling.

5. The missing pages in the ledger made the accounts an inadequate incomplete record of last month's business.

6. The project is finally finished and I have spent five busy challenging years working on it.

7. Our security measures include hourly checks by guards limited-access keys and video monitoring.

8. Howard's humor is not always clear to the rest of us; however he seems to have an enormous supply of quips puns and stories for all occasions.

9. As a sales representative I try to be personable and polite but I also try to maintain a professional distance.

10. Several companies may be willing to pay for the market research if the information is clear if the information is complete and if the information is valid.

11. Some supervisors will always be patient yet others are often curt with everyone.

12. Often the most careful writer will make obvious unnecessary editing mistakes.

13. The new mansion will have distinctive features including a walk-in refrigerator and a round swimming pool.

14. We will adopt the new procedure when we can get a new computer when we can find the right software and when we can find the right printer.

15. Ms. Tarner will help us with the project now but we will still need more time to work on it this summer.

The answers are in the back of the text-workbook.

LEARNING OBJECTIVES

After your study of Comma Rule 3, you will be able to:
- Insert commas correctly between introductory elements and the main sentence.
- Label comma uses to show that the introductory element is one of the following: noun of address, mild interjection, group of prepositional phrases, participial word or phrase, infinitive phrase, subordinate clause, absolute, or transition word or phrase.
- Insert and label commas accurately when the uses from Rules 1, 2, and 3 are mixed in sentences.

RULE 3: Use commas after INTRODUCTORY elements in sentences.

A. Nouns of address

B. Mild interjections (oh, well, my, ...)

C. Group of prepositional phrases
(in, on, over, under, through, of, ...)

D. Participial words or phrases

E. Infinitive phrases (*to* and a verb)

F. Subordinate clauses
(when, if, after, since, because, ...)

G. Absolutes

H. Transition words or phrases
(in summary, in conclusion, first of all, ...)

A. Karen, the door is still open.

B. Well, I didn't like the conference.

C. In a rush of anger without a second
thought, he destroyed the experiment.

D. Referring to the chart, you will note the
clear results of the research.

E. To install the storm door, remove the
packing material and the trim.

F. After he retyped the memo, Carlos sent it
to his boss.

G. Headlights piercing the fog, the
ambulance continued its course.

H. First of all, I want to explain the controls.

**Fold out the Compact Comma Summary in the back of the text-workbook so you can see it
while you read the explanations and work on the exercises.**

COMMA—INTRODUCTORY

A comma is used to separate an introductory element from the rest of the sentence. Several types of elements will fit in that introductory slot. Figure 1-5 shows the pattern.

FIGURE 1-5

The introductory structure

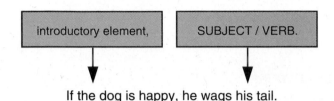

If the dog is happy, he wags his tail.

A. Nouns of address

When a sentence begins with a person's name and the person is directly addressed by the sentence, a comma must follow the name.

Ed, please close the door.

Dr. Fening, your photos are ready for pick up.

B. Mild interjections

Use a comma to separate mild interjections at the beginning of a sentence. Words such as *my, oh, yes,* and *no* are mild interjections and have commas placed after them.

Well, I guess you can borrow my car.

No, your order was not lost in the mail.

Yes, further investigation will be necessary.

C. Group of prepositional phrases

The first step in applying this rule is to recognize prepositional phrases. A prepositional phrase is a group of words beginning with a preposition from the following group:

of	up
in	on
over	under
by	beside
near	at
around	through
between	among
down	with

This is not a complete list. Other words will be used as prepositions at times. Almost every sentence has a prepositional phrase in it. Sample prepositional phrases include:

in the street	on the corner
around the bend	through the forest
near the old barn	at the baseball game
over the bridge	of little importance

Notice that each phrase begins with a preposition and then includes other words that complement it. Generally at the beginning of a sentence, commas do not follow these phrases. However, a comma should separate a group of these phrases from the beginning of the sentence.

For example, the sentence that follows has three phrases at the beginning.

> On a steaming day in mid-July in Louisiana, the humidity can almost be held in your hand.

> On a steaming day
> in mid-July
> in Louisiana

The sentence needs a comma because it has a group of three phrases. On the other hand, if only one phrase were used, the comma would not be necessary.

> On a steaming day the humidity can almost be held in your hand.

D. Participial words or phrases

Participles are the *-ing* form or the *-en/-ed/-t* form of a verb. The *-ing* form is the present participle, and the *-en/-ed/-t* form is the past participle. Use commas to set off a participle or a participial phrase at the beginning of a sentence.

Broken,	(participle)
Dashing,	(participle)
Broken in three places,	(participial phrase)
Dashing madly for the plane,	(participial phrase)
Stepping boldly to the front,	(participial phrase)
Pacified for the moment,	(participial phrase)

PRESENT PARTICIPLE. If you use the *-ing* form of a verb like *referring, running, jumping* at the beginning of a sentence, then separate it from the sentence with a comma. Use commas with participles or participial phrases that describe at the beginning of sentences.

> Running to catch the taxi, the businessperson dropped her briefcase.

In this sentence the phrase *Running to catch the taxi,* describes the businessperson and is therefore an adjective.

PAST PARTICIPLE. The past participle is the form of a verb used with the word *have.* Frequently the verb form ends in *-ed* like the regular past tense; occasionally it ends in *-en* or *-t.*

tried	broken
scooped	taken
worked	burnt

These words may be placed at the beginning of sentences and describe other words that follow. They are similar to -ing words.

> Broken in several places, the stained glass window was smashed beyond repair.

The phrase *Broken in several places* describes the stained glass window. Since it begins the sentence, include a comma according to Rule 3D.

The past participle and a helping word such as *having* may be used to show one action occurring before another.

> Having run hard, the athlete broke all records.

MISPLACED OR DANGLING MODIFIERS. When you place describing phrases *before* the words described as introductory elements of the sentences, use a comma. The first element after the comma must be the item described. If the described item is the wrong one, the modifier is misplaced. If the described item is missing, the modifier is dangling.

misplaced	Swimming in the milk pail, Uncle Jack noticed the small kitten.
dangling	Trying to complete the order on time, the two hours of overtime really paid off.

In the first sentence Uncle Jack is mistakenly the one swimming in the milk pail instead of the small kitten. In the second sentence *Trying to complete the order on time,* really does not describe anything else in the sentence. Here are corrected versions:

Correct	Uncle Jack noticed the small kitten swimming in the milk pail.
Correct	Trying to complete the order on time, the crew worked two hours overtime.

Written this way, the kitten is swimming, and the crew is completing the order. The modifiers are in the right places, and the items modified are clear.

E. Infinitive phrases

Use commas to set off infinitive phrases that are introductory modifiers. The infinitive phrase—a verb with the word *to* attached such as *to run, to jump, to live,* and *to work*—can be used as an adjective, an adverb, or a noun.

> To act compassionately, she shared her contest prizes with the other workers. (adjective)

> To eliminate waste, the manager started a recycling program. (adverb)

> To act with proper authority is the officer's job. (noun)

If the phrase describes, use a comma. If the phrase does not describe, do not use a comma.

> To run for office in his home state, the general had to resign his commission. (adjective/describes)

> To run a mile a day is good exercise. (noun)

F. Subordinate clauses

Subordinate clauses begin with a subordinating conjunction and have a subject and verb. These elements are now part of a larger sentence. These are subordinating conjunctions:

when	though	although
if	while	as
after	since	before
as if	because	

Begin with two short sentences, add one of the subordinate conjunction words, and then combine the sentences.

> The sun sets.

> The night will cool.

Select one of the words from the list. In this case *after* is a reasonable choice. Now add it to the first sentence.

> After the sun sets

> The night will cool.

Now you should notice that the first sentence seems unfinished. By adding the subordinate conjunction, you make one sentence rely on another sentence.

> After the sun sets, the night will cool.

With these combined sentences, called complex sentences, the comma follows the first clause. The main point is that the night will cool. The clause *after the sun sets* tells the condition for it to happen. The relationship is shown in Figure 1-6.

FIGURE 1-6

Subordinate clause followed by a main clause

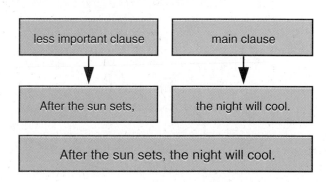

You also notice that the clauses could be written in the opposite order as shown in Figure 1-7. When the less important one follows, no comma is used.

FIGURE 1-7

Main clause followed
by the subordinate
clause

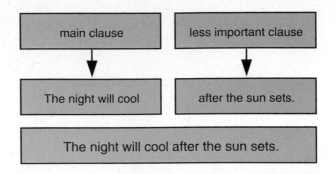

main clause	less important clause
The night will cool	after the sun sets.

The night will cool after the sun sets.

Some additional examples of sentences with subordinate clauses follow:

When the game is over, the team will celebrate.

If you finish the dishes, you will have time to watch television.

After you mow the lawn, you will be paid.

Because you have tried, your efforts will be rewarded.

Since the mail came early, we can finish by noon.

Although she worked hard, she could not meet the deadline.

G. Absolutes

Another phrase is the absolute construction. Even though many books do not mention it, an absolute is a phrase that is actually a sentence with some parts missing. Although these structures are usually used by some sophisticated writers, they can be effective for everyone.

His horse waiting close by, the scout studied the tracks.

Her hand reaching confidently for the racquet, the tennis pro began the last set.

These are describing phrases that use a noun and a describing verb form. They are neither clauses nor participial phrases. Think of them as another kind of describing phrase. They can be used before or after the word they describe. When they occur at the beginning of a sentence, use the comma.

H. Transition words or phrases

When the first element of a sentence is a transition or bridge between the ideas before it and those which follow, use a comma to suspend the reader. Transition words and phrases include:

First,	Furthermore,
In conclusion,	On the other hand,
Obviously,	In other words,
In summary,	As a result,
For instance,	For example,
However,	In addition,
In conclusion,	In fact,

These words begin the sentence and serve to connect the sentence to the earlier ideas in the piece of writing.

In summary, your recommendation cannot be accepted without available funds.

On the other hand, the proposed project has some excellent advantages.

For example, carbon monoxide may be a byproduct of the chemical reaction.

COMBINING RULES

Many sentences are more complicated. More than one comma may be involved, or the sentence with the introductory element may be in a second clause as shown in Figure 1-8. In this case the introductory material still gets a comma even though it introduces the second clause.

FIGURE 1-8
Introductory element—clause

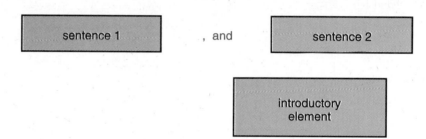

We do not want to buy any, and if you continue to call, we will seek help from an attorney.

In some cases the comma usage may become confusing for the reader. You may then rewrite the sentence for clarity or promote the compound sentence use from Rule 2A to a semicolon as shown in the following example:

We do not want to buy any; and if you continue to call, we will seek help from an attorney.

SUMMARY

The INTRODUCTORY uses of commas involve structures which introduce sentences. Include a comma to separate the introductory element. Use commas in the following introductory uses: nouns of address, mild interjections, groups of prepositional phrases, participial words or phrases, infinitive phrases, subordinate clauses, absolutes, and transition words or phrases.

EXERCISE 3A
Chapter 1   *COMMA*

RULE 3

- Insert commas in the following sentences and write the rule number and letter from the Compact Comma Summary above each comma you insert.
- All the uses involve only Rule 3.
- In the last five sentences one does not need commas.

Example: If all the runners are ready,³ᶠ the race can begin.

1. Elmer I told you we could not fix that now.

2. In conclusion the most difficult tasks are behind us.

3. If these pages are not printed by Friday the report will not be mailed on time.

4. Standing on the diving platform the Olympic diver prepared for her last dive in the series.

5. Yes you may go to the movie later this afternoon.

6. On the other hand you may have a good point.

7. In a case with several problems without answers the researchers must clarify the specific questions.

8. Dashing toward his waiting spaceship Buck Rogers fired at the approaching aliens.

9. After you have connected the retainer you must inspect it for a good fit.

10. Determined to make a good first impression Ana Maria headed from the parking lot toward her new job.

11. To gather all the information I will need to write several letters to many of our major customers.

12. Because the race was close the official announcement of the winner was delayed for half an hour.

13. The engine humming at idle the convertible was parked at the curbside while the campers were in the convenience store.

14. Carmella will be ready to depart at 7:00 a.m.

15. With all of the patents on past inventions I sometimes wonder how new items are even registered.

The answers are in the back of the text-workbook.

EXERCISE 3B
Chapter 1   *COMMA*

RULES 1–3

- Insert commas in the following sentences and write the rule number and letter from the Compact Comma Summary above each comma you insert.
- All the uses involve only Rules 1, 2, and 3.
- In the last five sentences one does not need commas.

Example: After the speaker completes the presentation,³ᶠ we will have time to recopy our detailed,²ᶜ complete notes.

1. Scurrying to finish before the bell rang the students in cooking class cleaned the counters replaced the pots and pans and washed the dishes in record time.

2. Gloria I told you that I did not want you to alter the schedule but I guess we can live with it now that the changes have been made.

3. If you do not like the way we do things around here you can leave; and you should take your grumbling sarcastic friend with you.

4. In summary your current operation is not large enough for additional employees; but a small computer an accounting software package and a word processing software package can increase the current employees' productivity.

5. Our final plans include an advertising campaign a benefit dance and 5,000 direct mail flyers.

6. We found the new clerk to be a well-mannered considerate person.

7. Meeting in secret for over three months the management of the company arranged for its merger.

8. Some employees find the work challenging rewarding and entertaining.

9. Oh I did not realize that you wanted to register for the class also.

10. Mr. Jones we hope that your order reaches you in time for the sale and we also hope that your new building will serve your growing company.

11. As the car coasted slowly to a stop the driver and passengers groaned in unison.

12. The report must include the cost price and quantity of each item on the order along with a concise clear description of the item.

13. The fire destroyed twenty of the thirty apartments in the building; no one was injured.

14. When the invoice is processed in our office we record all the amounts note the supplier's address and send the invoice to the accounts payable department.

15. Although you may not want to study the complicated detailed reports someone must make the decision.

The answers are in the back of the text-workbook.

28

LEARNING OBJECTIVES

After your study of Comma Rule 4, you will be able to:
- Insert commas correctly around interrupting elements.
- Label comma uses to show that the interrupting element is one of the following: noun of address, appositive, contrasting element, describing (but not necessary) phrase, describing (but not necessary) clause, absolute, or parenthetical expression.
- Insert and label commas accurately when the uses from Rules 1, 2, 3, and 4 are mixed in sentences.

RULE 4: Use commas to set off INTERRUPTING elements.

A. Nouns of address

A. In some cases, Mr. Mendez, this rule helps.
Close the window, Emma.

B. Appositives

B. The printer, a tractor mechanism, uses a simple control.
He bought a new car, a compact station wagon.

C. Contrasting elements

C. The software, not the hardware, is the problem in this case.
We remember our joys, not our sorrows.

D. Describing (but not necessary) phrases

D. The printed text, displayed with or without the coding, can be edited.
We enjoyed the new van, painted with a bright mural.

E. Describing (but not necessary) clauses

E. The line numbers, which apply in most cases, have limited value in this situation.
We can't go to Jessica's party, which will be held in a rented gym.

F. Absolutes

F. Matty McDougal, her fist clenching in anger, wanted only to be left alone.
Mark jumped at the sound of his alarm, its music blaring.

G. Parenthetical expressions

G. The program, admittedly, is weak in some areas.
She will finish the project, no doubt.
The accounts will be prorated; i.e., they will be adjusted.
We will ship all items (e.g., belts, slacks, and sweaters).

Fold out the Compact Comma Summary in the back of the text-workbook so you can see it while you read the explanations and work on the exercises.

COMMA—INTERRUPTING

The commas in Rule 4 deal with interruptions in the normal sentence flow. Several other punctuation marks can also interrupt sentences: dashes, parentheses, and ellipses (a series of three periods). The difference among them is the strength with which they interrupt the sentence.

The comma provides the mildest interruption. Generally these interrupting commas come in pairs to show where the regular sentence has been interrupted. The first comma of the pair indicates a break. The second comma indicates that the interruption is complete and the regular sentence will continue. The pattern is shown in Figure 1-9.

FIGURE 1-9

The Interrupting structure (internal)

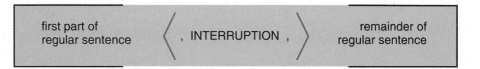

Several grammatical constructions fit in this interrupting slot. Something interrupts the main sentence, and that item has a comma on each end. Notice for this rule that the Compact Comma Summary has an additional feature, two examples for each rule. This is because the interruption sometimes occurs at the end of a sentence. In such cases the regular sentence is followed by a comma and an interrupting item as shown in Figure 1-10.

FIGURE 1-10

The Interrupting structure (at the end)

A. Nouns of address

Use a pair of commas to enclose an interrupting noun of address. This is the same use as the noun of address in Rule 3, but in this case the noun of address is in an interrupting position rather than in the introductory position.

> At last, Michael, you have finished the last problem.

> We included in your last order all the forms you requested, Mr. Komuro.

B. Appositives

Use a pair of commas to separate an appositive from the remainder of the sentence. An appositive is a noun that restates the noun just before it. Usually the second noun is more specific, or it provides additional information. One of the common patterns is to use a person's name and then follow it with the person's title as an appositive.

Mr. Byrd, the manager of the department, will be developing the guidelines.

The president, the only officer with the agenda, led the meeting with an iron hand.

Of course, these items could also occur at the end of the sentence.

We will complete the last step when it is approved by Ms. Olmstead, the project manager.

C. Contrasting elements

Use a pair of commas to separate interrupting contrasting elements. The contrasting elements are similar to the appositives. In one sense they refer back to the noun, but a contrasting element contradicts the idea that comes before it. In this situation use the word *not* and a second noun that means the opposite of the first noun.

The tables, not the chairs, must be moved before the meeting can begin.

We hope to capitalize on our hopes, not our fears.

He used his head, not his heart, when judging the entries.

D. Describing phrases

Use a pair of commas to separate optional interrupting phrases. The importance of the interrupting information makes a difference in comma usage. Acting like mild parentheses, the commas let the reader know that the information is optional. If the information is optional, put in the commas. If the information is necessary to the meaning of the sentence, leave out the commas.

The principal's office, located just inside the door, is off limits.

The car painted only with primer sat among the others in the garage.

E. Describing clauses

Use a pair of commas to separate interrupting clauses that are optional describers. The clauses usually begin with the words *who* or *which*. A similar construction is a clause beginning with the word *that,* but information with the word *that* is always needed and does not receive commas.

Miss Akita, who is a partner in the legal firm, will be available on Tuesday.

We will send Betty Alsop, who is the captain of the team.

This personal computer is the one that I ordered for the office.

When the interrupting information is at the end of a sentence, only one comma is needed.

OPTIONAL COMMAS.   Commas used with Rules 4D and 4E can be optional. Compare these two sentences:

> The girl who is standing in the corner is president of the club.

> Elvira Quidlash, who is standing in the corner, is president of the club.

Why does one sentence need two commas and the other one not need them? There is a person's name in the second sentence; therefore, the clause about standing in the corner is optional. In the first sentence the clause about standing in the corner is necessary to identify which girl; therefore, it has no commas.

F. Absolutes

An interrupting absolute has the same structure as an introductory absolute, but in this case it is in the middle or at the end of the sentence. Use commas to set off the absolute. Interrupting absolutes may be placed at the end of the sentence as well as in the middle interrupting position.

> He drove the battered pickup, the broken tailpipe rattling against the pavement, to the store in town.

> He drove to the store in town in the battered pickup, the broken tailpipe rattling against the pavement.

> Tom walked home, his head hung in sorrow, while others failed to notice.

> Others failed to notice Tom as he walked home, his head hung in sorrow.

G. Parenthetical expressions

Use a pair of commas to enclose interrupting parenthetical expressions. These expressions are used for politeness or to comment to the reader. When they interrupt at the ends of sentences, only one comma is necessary.

> You will, no doubt, finish the project on time.

> I have, admittedly, been late to the meeting before.

> Ms. Basker will allow some options, I am sure.

> He may not need all the time, of course.

When conjunctive adverbs (however, therefore, nevertheless, ...) are used as interrupters, put commas around these words when they are used in other positions in a sentence. Notice how the comma is used in the same sets of sentences from Rule 2B. When the semicolon is used, only one comma is appropriate. Not every sentence could be written with all three combinations; they might not all make sense. They may have slightly different meanings.

Beth will be the presiding officer at the meeting; however, the agenda is shorter than usual.

Beth will be the presiding officer at the meeting; the agenda, however, is shorter than usual.

Beth will be the presiding officer at the meeting; the agenda is shorter than usual, however.

Tony will not complete the draft; therefore, someone else will have to finish it.

Tony will not complete the draft; someone else will, therefore, have to finish it.

Tony will not complete the draft; someone else will have to finish it, therefore.

Commas set off another type of parenthetical word or phrase, the transitional expressions. Although similar to other parenthetical expressions, they really introduce additional words that expand the previous statement. The following expressions typically fit this category. Here are their meanings, abbreviations, and equivalents.

Latin term	Abbreviation	English equivalent
exempli gratia	e.g.	for example
id est	i.e.	that is or namely

They begin an interruption to the pattern of a sentence. The interruption itself restates the previous material by providing examples or repeating the information in another way.

Use a comma for a mild break in the sentence. A semicolon, a dash, and parentheses show stronger breaks. For examples of sentences with transitional expressions punctuated with semicolons, dashes, and parentheses refer to the chapters on those marks.

Remember that many readers today are not familiar with Latin. You will make a better style choice for communication if you choose the English equivalent.

The pattern for the project is set, i.e., the goals are clear to everyone.

The writer had called upon his old contact, namely, Bob Wilkens.

Generally a semicolon is used if the interrupting matter is a full clause.

His patience may be an obstacle for us; i.e., he may force us to wait longer for the financing for the project.

However, a comma always follows the transitional expression.

SUMMARY

Just like the **INTRODUCTORY** rule, the **INTERRUPTING** uses of commas involve a variety of structures. You are breaking the sentence's normal pattern for a moment to insert additional information that is usually optional. The commas are typically in pairs, one before and one after the interruption. Only one comma is used if the interruption occurs at the end of the sentence. Use commas to set off nouns of address, appositives, contrasting elements, optional describing phrases, optional describing clauses, absolutes, and parenthetical expressions.

EXERCISE 4A
Chapter 1   *COMMA*

RULE 4

- Insert commas in the following sentences and write the rule number and letter from the Compact Comma Summary above each comma you insert.
- All the uses involve Rule 4.
- In the last five sentences one does not need commas.

Example: The missing notes,^{4G} I believe,^{4G} will answer most of our questions.

1. With proper care Mrs. Phillips your new car should last well past 100,000 miles.

2. The chairs not the table must be moved first.

3. A careful study of our catalog provided for you at no cost will detail our complete product line.

4. The dealer will also provide financing and insurance for your new car a sports model with a sunroof.

5. The newest version of the program which was published last month has all of the revisions you requested.

6. Careful planning will I believe solve many of the problems associated with the new computer application.

7. Jack Naife the president of the local bank was just elected mayor.

8. The sales manager will consider all of your offers which are provided in our contract proposal.

9. The letter will be provided after the contract is signed i.e. after the agreement is official.

10. The protective cover mounted over the delicate connections is made of a heat-resistant material.

11. Most of the accounting problems which cannot be solved with a better calculator must be resolved through a close examination of the receipts.

12. Ms. Susan Harper the vice president of finance for the company will be presenting the annual report during the meeting.

13. You will find that your study of the text will be most helpful when you take this test.

14. James Cotter who is a consultant for both business and government office operations will provide us with a clearer picture of all the decision factors.

15. We cannot approve your application at this time; we will reconsider it in six months however.

The answers are in the back of the text-workbook.

EXERCISE 4B
Chapter 1   *COMMA*

RULES 1–4

- Insert commas in the following sentences and write the rule number and letter from the Compact Comma Summary above each comma you insert.
- The uses involve Rules 1, 2, 3, and 4.
- In the last five sentences one does not need commas.

Example: We will discuss our common memories,⁴ᶜ not our old grudges,⁴ᶜ at the reunion picnic,¹ᴬ dinner,¹ᴬ and dance.

1. Our club president will no doubt finish the project; and he will then turn over the office to another ambitious aspiring leader.

2. Visiting the hospital with her Aunt Jane Tina became interested in volunteer work herself.

3. Our new model offers many advantages over our competition and our older model e.g. lower initial cost higher efficiency and a longer time between scheduled maintenance checks.

4. Billy you need to apply another coat of paint to the doghouse but you will have to wait until we get more paint however.

5. Our goals and accomplishments not our fears and disappointments must govern our feelings of self-worth.

6. Those unfamiliar abbreviations a shortcut you use are very confusing for people who do not know them.

7. After the purchasing agent completes the requisition the order is immediately forwarded but you may not get the receipt for a few days.

8. Yes I think your plan will provide the advantage we need faster delivery time.

9. On the other hand we cannot ignore the new products provided by our innovative aggressive competitors.

10. John Steinbeck who is a famous writer most of us have encountered in school had many critics in his early years.

11. If you follow all of the steps you will be able to assemble the unit without a technician.

12. Without thinking about all the consequences of his actions the rodeo cowboy mounted the bronco and nodded for the gate to open.

13. The leader will need to show a solid plan a willingness to talk about it and the perseverance to repeat it several times.

14. Professor Davis will verify the calculations.

15. Tom Hector the author of the novel used the first three chapters to develop the situation and the characters a group of race car drivers.

The answers are in the back of the text-workbook.

STANDARD
Chapter 1   *COMMA*

LEARNING OBJECTIVES

After your study of Comma Rule 5, you will be able to:
- Insert commas correctly in standard places.
- Label comma uses to show that the standard usage is one of the following: between and after parts of an address (without ZIP codes), between and after parts of a date, in setting off the direct words of a speaker, in a business letter after the close, in a personal letter after the opening and the close, between and after titles, in an alphabetic listing of names, in the change of a statement into a question, or in numbers.
- Insert and label commas accurately when the uses from all five rules are mixed in sentences.

RULE 5: Use commas in STANDARD places.

A. Between and after parts of addresses in a sentence (without ZIP codes)

   A. San Francisco, California
     1000 Central Street, Dayton, Ohio
     He was born in Phoenix, Arizona, after the war.

B. Between and after parts of dates in a sentence

   B. January 15, 1988
     Saturday, June 19, 1971
     He won the race May 17, 1903, after many years of training.

C. In setting off the direct words of a speaker

   C. Joan said, "That is not true."
     "It is possible," Joan said, "to complete the job in an hour."
     "That can't be," Joan declared.

D. In a business letter after the close
E. In a personal letter after the opening and the close

   D. Sincerely,
   E. Dear Matthew,
     Your friend,

F. Between and after titles in a sentence

   F. William Phold, Jr., is the only son of William Phold, Ph.D.

G. In an alphabetic listing of names

   G. Graves, Debbie
     Roberts, Josh
     Shaker, James

H. In the change of a statement into a question
I. In numbers

   H. Teresa is the boss here, isn't she?
   I. 1,256
     421,226,500

Fold out the Compact Comma Summary in the back of the text-workbook so you can see it while you read the explanations and work on the exercises.

COMMA—STANDARD

Rule 5 covers all of the standard uses of commas. Do you remember learning about commas between cities and states and within dates? How about using commas with quotation marks? Tradition governs most Rule 5 commas uses. Rule 5 in the Compact Comma Summary is a quick, clear reference for putting commas in standard places.

A. Addresses

Always put commas between cities and states. If more of the sentence follows the state, put a comma after the state also. If you write the address on one line instead of stacking the elements, separate the major elements with commas. Do not separate the ZIP code from the state with a comma.

> Her office is in the same neighborhood at 314 Canton Drive, Lansing, MI 48917.

B. Dates

Separate the parts of a date with commas. If you use only the month and year, the comma is not necessary. If more of the sentence follows the date, place a comma after the year.

> May 5, 1992

> He signed the document on August 5, 1989, after studying it carefully.

> June 1990

C. Quotations

Use commas to separate the direct words of a speaker. When a comma follows a speaker's words, put the comma inside the second quotation mark. If the direct quotation is at the beginning or end of a sentence, only one comma will probably be necessary. If the quotation is interrupted by words such as *he said* or *Tom questioned*, then two commas will be needed.

> "Please cancel the order," Akemi said.

> Nancy replied, "I don't want to run for office."

> "We will proceed," Al said, "when the transfer is complete."

D. Business letter

When the salutation (a greeting such as *Dear Ms. Ross*) of a business letter ends with a colon, only the complimentary close (Sincerely yours) receives a comma.

> Ladies and Gentlemen: Dear Ms. Goddard:
>
> Cordially,   Sincerely,

E. Personal letter

A personal letter differs from a business letter. The salutation and the complimentary close of a personal letter are both followed by commas.

Dear Sherry,   My dear Aunt Wilma,

Very truly yours,   With love,

F. Titles

When you use titles *after* someone's name, a comma follows the name. A comma follows the title if more of the sentence follows. Notice the unusual situation where an abbreviation for a title ends in a period, and the comma directly follows. Use both the period and the comma in these situations.

Patricia Mosier, M.D.   Timothy S. Fening, Jr.

He gave the lecture in honor of Bernice Cable, Ph.D., who was the founder of the college.

The matter was taken to Malcolm Smith, Sr., since his son was out of town.

G. Alphabetic lists

When you write the names of people in reverse order, the comma lets the reader know that you have written the last name first.

Baxter, Christi

Holverson, Lana

Melendez, Roberta

H. Tag questions

When you convert a statement into a question by adding a couple of reversing words at the end, separate those reversing words with a comma. This is called a tag question.

We are finished with the job.
We are finished with the job, aren't we?

We will return to camp next year.
We will return to camp next year, right?

I. Numbers

Separate large numbers with commas between each set of three digits. No commas are necessary for numbers less than 1,000. Commas are always used with numbers larger than 9,999. Numbers with four digits (1,000 through 9,999) can be treated either way. In many cases they will follow the same pattern as other numbers around them. Use a comma when the other numbers do; drop the comma when you can.

451	444,999.03	1,234,555
234	1,345.87	34,566
6754		

Rule 5   STANDARD

SUMMARY

The **STANDARD** uses of commas are familiar. Use commas associ-, ated with dates and addresses, use them with direct quotations and titles, and use them in personal and business letters. Also use commas with lists of names in reverse order, use them when you change a statement into a question (as a tag), and use them to group digits in large numbers. Don't forget the commas that follow some of these items when used within sentences; these are often neglected.

EXERCISE 5A
Chapter 1 *COMMA*

RULE 5

- Insert commas in the following sentences and write the rule number and letter from the Compact Comma Summary above each comma you insert.
- All the uses involve only Rule 5.
- In the last five sentences one does not need commas.

Example: "We cannot finish by midnight unless,⁵ᶜ Becky replied,⁵ᶜ "we get extra help."

1. He will have to move to Chicago Illinois to accept the new job.

2. This is the last row of weeds isn't it?

3. My aunt said "Please come back for another visit soon."

4. Robert Tanaka M.D. will be the president of the association next year.

5. Dear Uncle Henry

   Thank you for the graduation gift. I plan to use it next year in college.

   Your youngest nephew
   Tom

6. The Declaration of Independence was signed on July 4 1776.

7. Dear Mr. Carlson:

   Your order will be processed immediately. We apologize for the delay.

   Sincerely
   Manuel Ramos Sales Manager

8. The report indicates sales of 104855 units last month.

9. "This practice should be stopped before the next court session" the judge declared.

10. The members of the committee included:

    Hollingshead Alison
    Schneider Candy

11. Dear Mr. Jones:

    Please consider my application for department clerk.

    Sincerely
    Amy Smith

12. We left our car in Houston Texas with a damaged engine.

13. The leaders from Portland Oregon signed a new agreement on August 12 1974.

14. Several cities were cited in 19— as outstanding for their work with new schools.

15. Beth Wilson Ph.D. spoke at the meeting on October 2 19—.

The answers are in the back of the text-workbook.

EXERCISE 5B
Chapter 1   *COMMA*

RULES 1–5

- Insert commas in the following sentences and write the rule number and letter from the Compact Comma Summary above each comma you insert.
- The uses involve all five comma rules.
- In the last five sentences one does not need commas.

Example: He had kept a copy of the contract since June 14,^5B 1947,^5B when it was originally signed,^5B but he did not want anyone to know about it.

1. After we complete this project^2A we will all have to find new jobs.

2. Running to catch the departing airliner the passenger dropped his luggage tag with his destination Cincinnati Ohio.

3. Tracy please stop saying "I don't want to go."

4. His offbeat opinions not his political opponents contributed to his loss in the recent election.

5. The judge will no doubt make her ruling later in the week but the implications of it may last for several years.

6. The meeting was held in Newark New Jersey on October 23 1976 to discuss the final details of the contract.

7. In conclusion let me say that I have enjoyed your pleasant congenial company.

8. Arthur Critick the journalist responsible for the article refused to reveal his sources.

9. We hope for excellent results from our goals for next quarter; i.e. we hope to increase productivity by 10 percent expand to two new markets and maintain low overhead costs.

10. The president of the humane society whom we all recognize as a fair person will make the final selection of an assistant manager.

11. The backers of the plan will require additional political support for the plan to have a chance.

12. "If the most qualified candidates are chosen we will have a well-balanced department" the chief indicated in the interview.

13. We will use block construction not frame walls for the three remaining new houses in this developed older neighborhood.

14. You were able to complete the problems but your answers were not accurate.

15. The letter was mailed to your address in Atlanta Georgia after you moved on July 12 19—.

The answers are in the back of text-workbook.

EXERCISE 5C
Chapter 1   *COMMA*

- Insert commas in the following letter and write the rule number and letter from the Compact Comma Summary above each comma you insert.
- The letter uses all five rules.
- Some sentences may have commas from several rules.

Peterson's Plastics
1089 East Juniper Lane
Logan UT 84321

January 13 19—

Mr. Phil Snidley President
Phamous Manufacturing
1111 West Cedar Drive
Davis CA 95616

Dear Mr. Snidley:

We have reviewed your proposal but our evaluation team has rejected it. In summary your proposal attacks the basic problem yet it neglects the practical matters associated with implementing the solution. You do not provide financial guidelines a realistic time frame or a staffing estimate. With your record of success Mr. Snidley we are somewhat disappointed.

If you care to revise your final offer please send it by January 31 19— to 234 Eastern Avenue Pasadena CA 91107. We cannot accept it after that date which is based on other corporate obligations. The extra work is worthwhile isn't it?

Sincerely

Mrs. Sally King Purchasing Agent

The answers are in the back of the text-workbook.

EXERCISE 5D

Chapter 1   *COMMA*

RULES 1–5

- Insert commas in the following memorandum and write the rule number and letter from the Compact Comma Summary above each comma you insert.
- The memo uses all five rules.
- Some sentences may have commas from several rules.

```
                      MEMORANDUM


           TO:  Bill Diamond
         FROM:  Clover Needhap
         DATE:  April 7 19—
      SUBJECT:  AB1 400 EVALUATION REPORT

In summary the AB1 400 unit is a quick reliable device; however
we are not happy with its price. Although we found some prob-
lems with the documentation all were easily overcome with only
minor revisions. The accompanying interface included at no
extra cost makes the system complete. The printer the interface
and the unit are all available from Cactus Computer Connections
1414 East Thirsty Circle Death Valley California 92328. If you
need additional information give me a call on Extension 667.
```

The answers are in the back of the text-workbook.

SEMICOLON

Chapter 2   The Mark In Between

The semicolon is an often misunderstood punctuation mark, yet its uses are fairly well prescribed. The semicolon is stronger than a comma, but it is weaker than a colon or an end mark such as a period, exclamation mark, or question mark. The semicolon has three major roles shown by the three key words in the Compact Semicolon Summary: **Connect**, **Clarify**, and **Introduce**. The following explanations, examples, and exercises detail these three purposes.

CONNECT
Chapter 2   *SEMICOLON*

LEARNING OBJECTIVES

After your study of Semicolon Rule 1, you will be able to:
- Insert semicolons correctly between clauses that need connecting.
- Label semicolon uses to show clause connections *with or without* additional connecting words.

RULE 1: Use semicolons to CONNECT independent clauses.

A. Compound sentence without conjunction

A. The game will start later; you have to prepare now.

B. Compound sentence with conjunctive adverb (however, therefore, moreover, nevertheless)

B. The final report is due Thursday; therefore, the figures from the computer must be ready Wednesday.

Fold out the Compact Semicolon Summary in the back of the text-workbook so you can see it while you read the explanations and work on the exercises.

SEMICOLON—CONNECTING

A. Compound sentences without conjunction

Use a semicolon to connect two or more independent clauses in a compound sentence. The semicolon is strong enough to connect two or more clauses without any other connecting words. Usually writers only join two clauses, but you may join more if you wish.

Sometimes you will want to join two related shorter sentences to make a longer compound sentence. When the meanings of the two shorter sentences have equal importance, you may simply join the two with a semicolon.

Think of the compound sentence as a balance with the semicolon as the pivot point. (See Figure 2-1.) The small sentences on each side are of equal value. Each side has a subject and a verb.

FIGURE 2-1

Two clauses connected by a semicolon

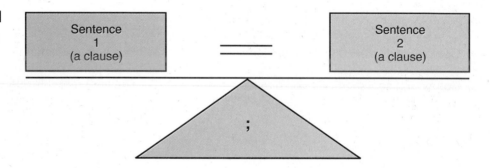

Look at the example sentence from the Semicolon Summary. You could write it as two short sentences like this:

The game will start later. You will have to prepare now.

Insert the semicolon, remove the period, and change the capital letter to lowercase.

The game will start later; you will have to prepare now.

In Chapter 1 you learned the comma and a conjunction such as *and, but,* or *or* can join sentences in the same way. The semicolon method is a way to show a more abrupt connection between the two ideas as well as to vary your sentences. Remember that the two ideas in any sentence joined in this way must be of equal value. The complete sentence should be balanced.

B. Compound sentence with conjunctive adverbs

Another way to connect two equal sentences is to join them with a semicolon and a special group of connector words called *conjunctive adverbs.* You will recognize this group of familiar words called conjunctive adverbs shown in Figure 2-2.

FIGURE 2-2

Conjunctive adverbs

therefore	then	thus
however	besides	likewise
furthermore	otherwise	consequently
moreover	also	meanwhile
nevertheless	anyhow	accordingly
hence	indeed	still
henceforth	instead	

A comma follows the conjunctive adverb when the semicolon joins clauses in a compound sentence. The overall structure of this combination is really the same as the structure in Rule 1A.

FIGURE 2-3

Two clauses connected by a conjunctive adverb

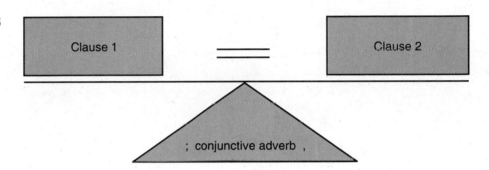

Study these two examples. Notice that the connecting unit has three parts: the semicolon, the conjunctive adverb, and the comma.

Marcia will be the presiding officer at the meeting; however, the agenda is shorter than usual.

Charles will not complete the draft; therefore, someone else will have to finish it.

The semicolon joins the sentences because the connecting words, the conjunctive adverbs, are not "strong" enough. The writer can move the conjunctive adverbs to other positions in the sentence. If the writer does rewrite with the words in other positions, he or she loses the connection the conjunctive adverb provides. The semicolon by itself makes the connection. That is why the careful writer chooses the semicolon.

SUMMARY

The semicolon *connects* independent clauses of equal importance in compound sentences with or without a conjunctive adverb. It is a stronger punctuation mark than a comma and a weaker one than a colon.

EXERCISE 1
Chapter 2   *SEMICOLON*

RULE 1

- Insert semicolons in the following sentences and write the rule number and letter from the Compact Semicolon Summary above each semicolon you insert.
- All the uses involve Rule 1.
- In the last five sentences one does not need a semicolon.

Example: The coach will resign at the end of the regular season*1A*; he will not manage the team in post-season play.

1. The order for Carlson Manufacturing is complete however, we cannot ship it until tomorrow.

2. All the fines have been paid your record is clear.

3. The conference call was cancelled therefore, we will also have to reschedule our planning meeting.

4. The handful of members at the meeting decided on the plan we all must now support it.

5. Our approach to the problem is more methodical however, we will still need a little inspiration.

6. Mr. Katz, the paper you submitted is acceptable however, you may wish to expand it later.

7. The sample illustrates the problem it does not confirm your proposed solution.

8. You will have several chances nevertheless, every one must be a wholehearted effort.

9. Glorious clouds swirled in the sky we watched in awe from the protection of the porch.

10. You can redeem the coupon however, you must make the purchase with cash.

11. My disorganized attempt to gather a consensus failed I will be more organized next time.

12. The 30-second commercial was scheduled for a time slot following the evening news therefore, the slot before the news is available.

13. Randall ran the race with the world record as his goal he failed to achieve it.

14. With a bold gesture the chairperson allowed one more motion however, that one motion called for two hours of debate.

15. You may be certain that the rules will always apply, yet they are not always enforced.

The answers are in the back of the text-workbook.

CLARIFY

LEARNING OBJECTIVES

After your study of Semicolon Rule 2, you will be able to:

- Insert semicolons correctly to clarify separations made with other punctuation.
- Label semicolon uses to show whether the separation is a series, a compound sentence, or a separation following a colon.

RULE 2: Use semicolons to CLARIFY separations with other punctuation.

A. Series with internal commas

A. She had lived in Denver, Colorado; Miami, Florida; and Sacramento, California.

B. Compound sentences with conjunction and internal commas

B. In conclusion, if Cleveland is not the site, Columbus may be an alternative; but I will not have the reports, plans, or arrangements ready for the meeting.

C. Series of clauses or long phrases following a colon

C. We will be making the following changes: the covers will be changed; the racks will be lifted; and our procedures will be rewritten.

Fold out the Compact Semicolon Summary in the back of the text-workbook so you can see it while you read the explanations and work on the exercises.

SEMICOLON—CLARIFYING

Semicolon uses that fall under Rule 2 involve the idea that some punctuation marks are stronger than others. A writer will use commas for one reason and then need additional commas for another reason. When these commas confuse the reader, use the stronger semicolon to clarify the meaning of the sentence. Punctuation is the writer's tool to show the relationships of the ideas.

A. Series with internal commas

Use commas to separate the items in a series.

> He brought sandwiches, soda, and chips to the picnic.

The three items—sandwiches, soda, and chips—are separated by commas.

What does the writer do if the items themselves have standard commas in them? One example involves cities and states. If you have to write a series of cities and their states, you normally put commas between each city and state. The reader may get lost if you separate the three main items and the cities and states with commas. The sentence would look like this:

> For the trip we will be traveling to Houston, Texas, Wichita, Kansas, and Denver, Colorado.

The reader will slow down even if the meaning is obvious. The problem is worse when sentences contain series of items more complex than simply cities and states.

The solution to the problem is to use semicolons between each item of the series when the items themselves have commas. As you apply this punctuation rule, the structure of the sentence becomes clearer.

> For the trip we will be traveling to Houston, Texas; Wichita, Kansas; and Denver, Colorado.

In this way semicolons separate the main items, and the commas make the separations within the items. The hierarchy of punctuation clarifies the situation. By using a stronger punctuation mark (the semicolon) between the items, the writer shows the intended structure.

B. Compound sentences

Semicolon Rule 2B is a solution to a slightly different problem with commas and semicolons. In a compound sentence a comma and a coordinating conjunction separate the two independent clauses. The writer may be faced with the problem of what to do if the clauses themselves also have commas. This example sentence shows the problem.

> We will, Mr. Jackson, seek an alternative, but it also must be within the budget, meet the schedule, and pass the tests.

Commas surround the interrupting noun of address—*Mr. Jackson*. The writer also uses commas for a series in the second independent clause. With all this comma usage the reader may have difficulty seeing the connection joining the two clauses to make a compound sentence. Again, the solution is to replace the comma that connects the compound sentence with the stronger semicolon.

> We will, Mr. Jackson, seek an alternative; but it must also be within the budget, meet the schedule, and pass the tests.

USAGE NOTE.   You must use some judgment here. Some more traditional sources say that whenever even one comma is used, a semicolon is required. Other more modern authorities say that the semicolon is required only if the reader might be confused by the complexity. The writer must decide which punctuation is needed to make the meaning of the sentence clear.

C. Separation

When a colon introduces the items in a series, the semicolon is sometimes used to separate the items. The following example illustrates this rule.

> The new manager made several changes: she bargained for new wage structures; she combined job classifications; and she developed new review guidelines.

Notice how the semicolons separate the series of items. If the items were a simple list of words, commas would do to separate them. If the items themselves contained commas, the writer would need to use semicolons to separate the items.

SUMMARY

The semicolon can clarify relationships between sentence parts. It is stronger than the comma and weaker than the colon. The semicolon may clarify a series of items having internal commas, a compound sentence having multiple commas, or a series of major items following an introductory colon.

EXERCISE 2A

RULE 2

Chapter 2   *SEMICOLON*

- Insert semicolons in the following sentences and write the rule number and letter from the Compact Semicolon Summary above each semicolon you insert.
- All the uses involve Rule 2 only.
- In the last five sentences one does not need a semicolon.

Example: We will need to plan our route to include Cincinnati, Ohio; St. Louis, Missouri; and Denver, Colorado.

1. If you do not feel like a competent, confident leader, you will not show leadership to others yet those others will look for someone's lead to follow.

2. We will need to confirm reservations in all of the listed cities: Chicago, Illinois Pittsburg, Pennsylvania and Newark, New Jersey.

3. We cannot always recognize, control, or eliminate the fear of public speaking yet we can write in a protected, private environment.

4. Before we begin the project we must interview Sam Dillion, the finance manager Susan Castillo, the director of marketing and Charles Aiken, the retired planning manager.

5. During his first one hundred days in office President Franklin D. Roosevelt made several bold moves: he changed the way people looked at government work he spoke to the people directly about the problems and he demanded support from Congress.

6. Although we have made our selection for this supervisory position, you will find that other opportunities will soon be available yet you must compete with other capable, experienced individuals.

7. For warranty service the following conditions are required: authorized factory dealers must complete the repairs you must insure shipping and you must complete the registration.

8. On May 18, 1992, the manager completed the overbudget, overdue project but the months of effort exhausted him.

9. Jim will find the only way is to make changes: he will have to promote the right people he will have to select new people who will get results and he will need to set some clear goals for them to pursue.

10. The computer and printer were thoroughly tested: we ran the software with sample data we printed all twelve of the reports and we rechecked a sample of the calculations by hand.

11. My reservations about the proposal involve the required labor hours, the details of the maintenance agreement, and the need for an alternate power source.

12. If you are awarded the contract, Miss Davis, you will need to refurbish the old building, which is in an older district plan for new highway access, which also will be an expensive aspect of the project and develop an acceptable schedule.

The answers are in the back of the text-workbook.

EXERCISE 2B
Chapter 2   *SEMICOLON*

RULES 1–2

- Insert semicolons in the following sentences and write the rule number and letter from the Compact Semicolon Summary above each semicolon you insert.
- The uses involve Rules 1 and 2.
- In the last five sentences one does not need a semicolon.

Example: You must begin to project the right image; *1A* your promotion depends on it.

1. Patient strength can overcome doubt impatient anger may force the wrong action.

2. Older methods have proven themselves through the test of time however, innovation can make them more efficient.

3. For an alternate site you could consider these cities: Boston, Massachusetts Atlanta, Georgia or Charleston, South Carolina.

4. We can make the needed changes in the plan however, the date the project is finished will also change.

5. The physician moved quietly through the rooms and halls as she made her morning rounds all patients were making progress.

6. Masterfully compiling statistic after statistic, the baseball announcer prepared for the playoff game therefore, when the team was ready to take the field, he spoke to the radio listeners with authority about the team's history.

7. With the prototypes of his invention firmly in hand, Calvin began the process of testing including a variety of tests: electromagnetic interference to make sure it would not cause problems with neighbors cold temperature operation to make certain that it would work in the cold winters of Minnesota and endurance tests to determine how long it would actually last in operation.

8. Proper accounting methods can solve many financial problems of a new business no substitute will do.

9. The fascinating feature of the new building is the way that the elevator is visible from the outside and provides a beautiful view for the riders.

10. A critical manufacturing process can be changed only when all the variables have been considered: the costs of new equipment and servicing it the long-term facilities impact in terms of changes in square footage and associated mechanical changes and labor impact including not only the time involved but the fatigue of workers.

11. We will not develop the alternate plan now therefore, the need for an additional building and office space is not necessary.

12. Another way of looking at the problem, Ms. Smiley, is that we can meet all your requirements without any additional cost but you must agree to allow some flexibility in your demanding, accelerated schedule.

The answers are in the back of the text-workbook.

INTRODUCE
Chapter 2 *SEMICOLON*

LEARNING OBJECTIVES

After your study of Semicolon Rule 3, you will be able to:
- Insert semicolons correctly with Latin abbreviations which are transitional expressions.
- Insert semicolons correctly with the English equivalents of Latin abbreviations which are transitional expressions.
- Label semicolon uses to show the appropriate transitional expression.

RULE 3: Use semicolons to optionally INTRODUCE added details within transitional expressions with a formal break.

(Commas, colons, parentheses, and dashes may be used also. The semicolon provides a more formal or major break than a comma but a less formal break than a colon.)

minor break . . . . major break

,   ;   :   ( )   —

A. Introduce examples
   e.g. (*exempli gratia*) for example

A. Do not use periods with abbreviations for agencies because they are so common; e.g., FBI, CIA, or DOD.
   Do not use periods with abbreviations for agencies because they are so common; for example, FBI, CIA, or DOD.

B. Introduce words that clarify or restate
   i.e. (*id est*) that is or namely

B. Security guards will provide protection; i.e., they will be guarding the door and escorting people to their cars.
   Security guards will provide protection; that is, they will be guarding the door and escorting people to their cars.

Fold out the Compact Semicolon Summary in the back of the text-workbook so you can see it while you read the explanations and work on the exercises.

SEMICOLON—INTRODUCE

Rule 3 shows the use of semicolons with transitional expressions. Transitional expressions begin an interruption to the pattern of a sentence. The interruption itself restates the previous material by providing examples or repeating the information in another way.

The example sentences in the Compact Semicolon Summary show the same sentence using different Latin phrases and their English equivalents. When making your style choice, remember that many readers today are not familiar with Latin.

The semicolon is one of several punctuation options to use before the transitional expression. If you want a weak break in the sentence, use a comma. If you want a stronger break, use a dash. The hierarchy of punctuation is shown on the scale in Figure 2-4 and on the Compact Semicolon Summary. For examples of sentences with transitional expressions punctuated with commas, dashes, and parentheses, refer to the chapters on those marks.

FIGURE 2-4

Hierarchy of punctuation

weaker or minor break . . . . stronger or major break

,	;	:	( )	—
comma	semicolon	colon	parentheses	dash

A. Introduce examples

Use semicolons with transitional expressions to introduce examples.

> Do not use periods with abbreviations for agencies because they are so common; for example, FBI, CIA, or DOD.

The writer provides specific examples of abbreviations for *agencies*, which was the general term used in the first part of the sentence. The list begins with a semicolon and then the phrase *for example* followed by the examples themselves. Note that the writer could have chosen to use the Latin abbreviation instead of the English phrase.

B. Introduce words that clarify or restate

Use semicolons with transitional expressions to introduce additional words that restate the previous statement.

> The manager is handling the problem; i.e., she will refund your money.

The words that follow the transitional expression restate more specifically how the manager is handling the problem. The English equivalent is also acceptable.

SUMMARY

In Rule 3 the writer must make a choice whether a semicolon is the most appropriate punctuation mark to introduce an explanation, restatement, or series of examples. The semicolon rule is the same whether you use the Latin abbreviation or English equivalent. As the writer you must take care that you know the meaning you wish to relate and that your reader will easily understand your usage.

EXERCISE 3A
Chapter 2   *SEMICOLON*

RULE 3

- Insert semicolons in the following sentences and write the rule number and letter from the Compact Semicolon Summary above each semicolon you insert.
- All the uses involve Rule 3 only.
- In the last three sentences one does not need a semicolon.

Example: The oldest elements of the curriculum *3A* ; for example, Latin study and philosophy, should be evaluated in the next year.

1. The concerns for our meeting i.e., the budget for next year and the schedule for projects, must be discussed thoroughly before we make the final decisions.

2. Several of the reasons we approved the purchase that is, the advantages we saw at the time, have not shown actual improvement in operation.

3. You may cover all the material in your presentation that is, you may even cover the material that is normally only shown to your department.

4. When the mistakes are obvious e.g., missing letters, incorrect spacing, or crooked text, both the editor and the printer are at fault.

5. Patience with the new computer program in the face of frustration that is, waiting until your skill matches your desire for the program to work, will serve you in the long run.

6. To become even reasonably proficient, beginning tennis players must work on several skills at the same time i.e., serving, volleying, forehand strokes, and backhand strokes.

7. No complaints will be aired at the meeting that is, they will not be discussed openly.

8. All along the trail the hikers found evidence of many people using the trail i.e., paper litter, beverage cans, and a well-worn path with no vegetation.

9. You will probably not find any software that is available for that outdated computer model.

10. You may not use statistical techniques that are unfamiliar to your novice audience e.g., standard deviation, margin of error, and degree of confidence.

The answers are in the back of the text-workbook.

EXERCISE 3B   RULES 1-3
Chapter 2   *SEMICOLON*

- Insert semicolons in the following sentences and write the rule number and letter from the Compact Semicolon Summary above each semicolon you insert.
- The uses involve all the semicolon rules.
- In the last three sentences one sentence does not need a semicolon.

Example: The home team players will take the field as soon as the visitors complete their
            infield practice ; that may take another fifteen minutes.
                         1A

1. If you do not complete the project on time, your supervisor will not be pleased however, the customer will accept a delayed delivery.

2. The district sales offices will be moved to San Francisco, California St. Louis, Missouri and Newark, New Jersey.

3. Later in the month we will be conducting a complete inventory i.e., we will count the stock in every storage bin and workstation.

4. Many students find math a difficult subject others find it fascinating and learn easily.

5. All of the following alterations will be made before the end of the month: the storage racks will be moved the new lighting will be installed and the furniture will be replaced.

6. Businesses use a variety of advertising media including magazines, TV, and radio but their results vary because they target dramatically different markets.

7. We must complete all of the preparations for the meeting that is, we must be ready with a complete agenda and adequate facilities.

8. The data you requested confirm the conclusion moreover, the report adds enough information that others can study the problem.

9. Historically the president has served as a balance of power to the other branches however, in today's environment these traditional roles have changed.

10. The total shipment is ready that is, the inspections are complete and the units are packaged in their crates.

11. Metric units of measure will be used for the projected development of the new space probe namely, all specifications and requirements will use these units.

12. Proofreaders will not like the newer system of marking the copy because it will not use symbols with which they are familiar.

13. We will hold a conference with the following main officers: Carl Pastor, director of marketing Samantha Colter, vice president of sales and Susan Talmut, director of public relations.

14. How will we answer the budget questions i.e., what will be our rationale for the requests?

15. Coach Johnson is losing his patience he is beginning to pace on the sidelines.

The answers are in the back of the text-workbook.

COLON

Chapter 3 The Cordial Host

The colon situations vary almost as much as the comma uses. Some are mechanical tools to signal the reader while others demand the writer make choices about style and meaning. Two principles govern colon use. Writers use the colon to *separate* items for clarity. A familiar example is when a colon separates the hours and minutes when expressing time. The Compact Colon Summary Rules 1 and 2 detail these short and long mechanical separations. Rule 3 is about mechanical uses in correspondence.

The second principle requires the writer to make choices. Colons serve to *introduce, point to,* or *anticipate* information which follows them. This added information can be a quotation, restatement, optional information, or added details. Instead of separating as in the first principle, the colon acts to connect items based on meaning rather than mechanical separation. In some cases the correct punctuation will always be a colon. In other cases other punctuation marks may be acceptable, but the colon is more formal than its weaker counterparts.

MECHANICAL SEPARATION (SHORT ITEMS)
Chapter 3   *COLON*

LEARNING OBJECTIVES

After your study of Colon Rule 1, you will be able to:
• Insert colons correctly as mechanical separations between short items.
• Label colon uses with the type of short items being separated.

RULE 1: Use colons for Mechanical SEPARATION (SHORT items).

A. Hours and minutes
B. Biblical chapter and verse
C. Title and subtitle

D. Proportions (ratios)

A. 9:45 p.m.   6:30 a.m.
B. James 2:4   Exodus 12:1–10
C. *Punctuation: An Introduction*
   Columbus: A Man of His Times

D. 3:2   13:1

Fold out the Compact Colon Summary in the back of the text-workbook so you can see it while you read the explanations and work on the exercises.

COLON—SEPARATION (SHORT)

A. Hours and minutes

When you express time, separate the hours and minutes with a colon. Do not use any additional spaces between the colon and the digits.

7:45 a.m.   9:30 p.m.   11:20 a.m.

USAGE NOTES. The *a.m.* and *p.m.* notations are written in lowercase letters with periods and no spaces. If you use the words *morning, afternoon* or *evening* with a time, then *a.m.* and *p.m.* abbreviations should not be used. (Example—I will pick you up in the morning at 7:15.)

B. Biblical references

The colon separates the chapter and verse of biblical references.

Genesis 2:21   John 3:16   Matthew 4:21

If the reference includes a group of verses within a chapter, use a hyphen to show the range. If the reference continues between chapters, then both references are separated with a colon.

Mark 3:21–25 (verses within the same chapter)
Mark 3:21– 4:12 (verses spanning two or more chapters)

C. Titles and subtitles

Colon Rule 1C shows division of titles. A general or short title is often followed by a longer explanation or expansion called a subtitle.

The Powerful Beginners: Graduates of the Business Schools

Running: A Beginner's Guide to Exercise

On a book cover these titles may not be separated by a colon. Often the main title and the subtitle will be in different type styles, sizes, or colors. When you include them in sentences in your writing, you must include the colon.

D. Proportions or ratios

A colon is used to separate the parts of a proportion or ratio. The colon substitutes for the word "to." For example, "She won the election by a 3 to 2 margin." The more mathematical method of showing the relationship is 3:2. Use a colon to separate the parts of the ratio. A written ratio of 4:1 is pronounced "four to one."

SUMMARY

The colon, as shown in Rule 1, is used to separate the parts of some short items including hours and minutes, biblical chapters and verses, titles and subtitles, and parts of proportions.

EXERCISE 1
Chapter 3 *COLON*

RULE 1

- Insert colons in the following sentences and write the rule number and letter from the Compact Colon Summary above each colon you insert.
- All the uses involve Rule 1.
- In the last five situations one does not need a colon.

Example: We will leave for the trip at 6:45 a.m. sharp.

1. We will not be able to attend the meeting tomorrow at 315 p.m.

2. While he was in Europe, Frank Pastor wrote the book *George Patton General and Leader.*

3. The Reds outscored the Mets during the season 32.

4. The minister took her sermon from Mark 423.

5. The leader of the group began the study series, *Job's Troubles A Perspective for Troubled Times,* with a look at the first section of chapter one, Job 11–23.

6. Without complete cooperation we will not get done before the deadline, which is your meeting at 230 p.m.

7. The radio announcer completed the program, "We'll have more music until the hour of three."

8. Although the community leaders were working hard, they were not able to change the voter registration beyond the 51 proportion of eligible voters to registered ones.

9. The parable of the Good Samaritan, to which she frequently referred, is in Luke 1030–37.

10. With great fanfare the publishers launched the new magazine, *Presents Your Guide to Giftgiving.*

The answers are in the back of the text-workbook.

MECHANICAL SEPARATION (LONG ITEMS)
Chapter 3   *COLON*

LEARNING OBJECTIVES

After your study of Colon Rule 2, you will be able to:
- Insert colons correctly as mechanical separations between long items.
- Label colon uses with the type of long items being separated.

RULE 2: Use colons for Mechanical SEPARATION (LONG items).

A. Salutation and text of a speech

    A. Mr. Chairman, Miss Spencer, members of the club: thank you for inviting me to speak this evening.

B. Resolution and following statement

    B. Resolved: The legislature should plan for new schools.

C. Speaker and lines in a play or script

    C. Bob: I can't believe you.
    Sam: You don't have a choice.

D. Publishing mechanics
- Journal citation from volume (short form) Separates volume number from page.
- Place and publisher

- Separate acts and scenes of plays

    D.
- Williams, Julie. "Recovering from Loss," *Helping Hand,* 62:57–59, September 1989.
- Carbunkle, Amanda. *Hail to the Chef.* New York: Gourmet Publishing Company, 1988.
- Romeo and Juliet III:ii

Fold out the Compact Colon Summary in the back of the text-workbook so you can see it while you read the explanations and work on the exercises.

COLON—SEPARATION (LONG)

The long mechanical separations in Colon Rule 2 involve items that can be separated with a colon.

A. **Salutations in speeches**

If you are writing the text of a speech, separate the salutation from text of the speech with a colon. Use it if you have a list of people whom you are addressing as in this example:

> Mr. President, Members of the Board, and guests: please let me begin this evening with a short story. Once a young woman . . .

The colon separates the introduction or salutation from the speech text more clearly than another comma.

B. **Resolutions**

The colon formally introduces the resolution statement that follows it. This language is often used in clubs, organizations, boards, committees, or other situations to state clearly and perhaps "legally" the intention of the group. These resolutions are discussed or debated by the membership of the organization before they are official statements of the group.

> Resolved: The funding for the new development program will be based on a new vote by the members and the opinion research poll.

The colon separates the word *resolved* from the statement of resolution itself.

C. **Writing material for a play or script**

Use colons according to Colon Rule 2C if you are writing a script. As you develop the dialogue, use a colon to separate the name of the character who is speaking from the lines.

> Todd: Why can't we stay for the whole party?
>
> Mary: I told you we wouldn't have time even if we cut the visit short.
>
> Todd: Yeah, I know. But do we really have to leave now?
>
> Mary: Unfortunately, we do.

This method saves the writer from writing so many quotation marks. If you write screenplays or scripts often, you will find standards about typing them in guide books on screen writing or script writing.

D. **Bibliographies and references**

Colon Rule 2D shows the mechanics of punctuating references in footnotes and bibliographies. Refer to a specific style guide if you are sending your work to a publisher or meeting specific requirements. Some situations in notes and bibliographies use colons consistently. Magazines and journals are published in volumes. This number is not the month or week it is published. It is the volume number of the bound version when several issues are collected in a library. In this entry *17* is the volume number, separated by a colon from *26–27* which are the page numbers.

> Barnacle, William. "Life at Sea," *Seafarers' Quarterly* 17:26–27, August 1977.

Another use for the colon is with book entries. These notes include the city where the book is published and the publishing company. The place and publisher are separated by a colon.

> Smith, Jane. *My Time in Court.* New York: Biography Publishing Company, 1989.

Your style manual may vary slightly but these two rules are common.

Colons separate the references to acts and scenes in plays. For example, you might refer to lines by Shakespeare in *Henry V* II:i, which would be Act II, scene 1 of the play.

SUMMARY

The colon separates long and short items. The longer items (salutations, resolutions, names and lines, and publishing mechanics) complement the uses of colons with shorter items. Together these rules show how the colon indicates separations of parts for readers.

EXERCISE 2A
Chapter 3   *COLON*

RULE 2

- Insert colons in the following examples and write the rule number and letter from the Compact Colon Summary above each colon you insert.
- All the uses involve Rule 2.

Example: Mr. President, Members of the Committee, and our special guests **2A**: I want to thank each of you for attending our workshop . . .

1. Resolved The Symphony Support Organization (SSO) will provide half of the funding for the new concert hall.

2. Tammy   Be sure to call when you get to the ranch.

   Thom   OK, but it won't be before next week.

   Tammy   Thanks, I'll wait for the call.

3. Madame Chairman and members of the board I would like to nominate James Castle for next year's president.

4. Tina Barker   No, I will not go with you unless you change your clothes first.

   Vinny Barker   Sure, just because you don't approve of the color of my shirt, I have to change it.

   TB   It's not just me. That color is awful.

   VB   Well, I like it.

5. Patterhoff, Patricia. *Open to the Public*. San Francisco Porpoise Publishing, 1990.

6. We will now take a break before studying *Hamlet* III ii.

7. Mr. President, Mr. Peters, friends, and family you have selected me for this honor, and I thank you with all my heart.

8. Arthur   We can't finish by the deadline!

   Pam   We have to; the trucks won't wait.

9. Castle, Brenda. *Patience in the Face of Danger*. Newark Alternative Press, 1993.

10. Delanty, Robert, "The Effects of Amino Acids on Digestion of Fructose," *Journal of Nutritional Science*, 1 12–55, November 1993.

The answers are in the back of the text-workbook.

EXERCISE 2B
Chapter 3　　*COLON*

RULES 1–2

- **Insert colons in the following examples and write the rule number and letter from the Compact Colon Summary above each colon you insert.**
- **The uses involve Rules 1 and 2.**
- **In the last five situations one does not need a colon.**

Example:　　The pastor said, "Please open your Bibles to Mark 4*1B*: 21."

1. Resolved The Library Development Board will establish a fund to assist with the acquisition of additional materials for student research.

2. Thomas　　　We can't find the lost keys, Patty.

   Patty　　　But you won't need them if the door is unlocked.

3. When Albert Frances spoke at the luncheon, he read from his new book *After the Gold Rush California History in the 1860's*.

4. Your odds of success are only 32, which is not enough for a favorable vote.

5. Madame President, members of the club, and guests I find it fitting that we should meet today near the location of this historical event.

6. Kathy, the bus will depart promptly at 730 a.m.; the driver will not wait.

7. Killjoy, Francine. "Older Americans Find Happiness," *The Reporter*, 23 55–59.

8. Resolved The members of the executive committee will vote to approve the content of the annual report which will be titled *Lifeline A Report to the Hospital Shareholders*.

9. We will not wait past 630 p.m. for her to return from the errand.

10. Mr. Chairman, fellow delegates, and visiting students Making a speech this evening will not complete my assignment; it will only serve...

11. BK　　　Hold it! Our payroll is in that strongbox.

   TG　　　Too bad. Hand it over anyway.

12. Our chances of finishing the project by the deadline are only 41.

13. After the priest began the lesson everyone knew he was talking about John 316.

14. You can find the information in the bibliography.

   Paquette, William. *All is Will.* New York Dieters Publishing, Inc., 1989.

15. As members of the delegation and guests, we are entitled to hear the additonal remarks of the speaker without an additional fee.

The answers are in the back of the text-workbook.

CORRESPONDENCE MECHANICS
Chapter 3   *COLON*

LEARNING OBJECTIVES

After your study of Colon Rule 3, you will be able to:
• Insert colons correctly in the mechanics of correspondence.
• Label colon uses to show which correspondence use is appropriate.

RULE 3: Use colons in CORRESPONDENCE mechanics.

A. Author and typist's initials
B. Salutation from business letter
C. Carbon copy or photocopy notations

D. Memo headings and information

E. Subject line in letter

A. KJE:jb (letters and memos)
B. Dear Ms. Slater:
C. cc: William Gold
   pc: Maria Reeves
D.   To: Jim Simpson
   From: Kim Lee Chin
   Date: June 14, 19--
   Subject: Budget Projections
E. Subject: Your Request for Information

Fold out the Compact Colon Summary in the back of the text-workbook so you can see it while you read the explanations and work on the exercises.

COLON—CORRESPONDENCE

Writers of business letters and memos use colons in specific situations. Readers expect them. Your writing should reflect these standard rules of correspondence mechanics.

A. Initials

In business correspondence separate the author's and the typist's initials with a colon. The initials usually follow below the signature and provide a record of who wrote or dictated the correspondence and who prepared the document. The author's initials are listed first in all capital letters followed by a colon and the typist's initials in all lowercase letters.

In this example Kathy Jones has dictated the letter that was typed by her secretary, Thomas Flagon.

```
   . . . thanks for your help.

   Sincerely,


   Kathy E. Jones

   KEJ:tf
```

While this information is not useful to the receiver of the letter, it has value for the sender's records. It may prove useful if a follow-up phone call is needed. If only the typist's initials are on the letter, no colon will be required.

The custom of including initials in a letter may someday disappear or change. People are composing, keying, printing, and sending their own correspondence with the use of computers and other electronic equipment and software. The colon use may change to reflect the electronic file name, which stores the copy of the correspondence. Even so, some system like this will remain for recordkeeping, and the colon will likely remain a part of that system.

B. Salutations

Another standard use of the colon is following the salutation of a business letter. Follow the salutation with a colon.

```
Dear Sir:
Dear Mr. Diaz:
Dear Mrs. Quigley:
Dear Susan:
Gentlemen:
```

Use this rule for business letters with a punctuation style commonly called "standard" or "mixed" punctuation.

C. Copy notation

A third way the colon is used in letters is the copy note following the signature block. The letters *cc* for carbon copy or *pc* for photocopy and an individual's name are included. This note tells the receiver that a copy has been sent to someone else for information. Some style guides suggest simply using the letter *c* to show that a copy was sent to another person.

Although some style guides say that this use is optional, the Compact Colon Summary includes it because the summaries are complete.

```
. . . Please stay in touch.

Sincerely,

Thomas Told

pc: Harold Watkins
    Susan Arthur
```

D. Headings

This colon use involves memos rather than letters. Although the exact form of memos varies among organizations, the use of headings is consistent. The following example shows a form where no special stationery or organization form exists. Always separate the information from the heading with a colon. The order may vary somewhat on some forms, or abbreviations may be used.

```
      To:  Rebecca Soto
    From:  Lu-yin Shen
    Date:  12/18/--
 Subject:  Budget Requests for 19--
```

E. Subject lines

The last mechanical use of a colon in business correspondence is in the subject line of a letter. If a letter has a subject line following the salutation, include a colon, two blank spaces, and the topic of the letter.

```
Miss Norma Janes
1234 West 44th Street
Phoenix, AZ 85011

Dear Miss Janes:

Subject: Your Request for Information

Although we are concerned about your problem, we
are not able to extend a refund to you at this
time. We are . . .
```

The word *Reference* or the abbreviation *RE* may be substituted for the word *Subject,* and a colon would be used in the same way.

```
RE: Follow-up Information
```

SUMMARY

The third major colon rule is for business correspondence. Standards differ for business, government, and legal correspondence, but some rules are consistent. Follow the style conventions within your organization if it has specific guidelines.

Letter writers may use colons to separate the salutation from the body of the letter or to separate the author's and typist's initials. Writers may also use a colon to separate the notation for a copy (cc or pc) from the name of the person receiving the copy. Memo writers use a colon to separate the headings from the information itself. If a subject line is included in a letter, the word *Subject* is separated from the information with a colon.

EXERCISE 3A
Chapter 3   *COLON*

RULE 3

- Insert colons in the following material and write the rule number and letter from the Compact Colon Summary above each colon you insert.
- All the uses involve Rule 3.
- In the last five situations one does not need a colon.

Example: Sincerely,
                  Audrey Parsons
                  AP: bmh
                     3A

1.   To   Carl Samson
       From   Sally Alvarez
       Date   3/7/--
    Subject   Vacation Schedule

    Since summer is just around the corner, please have everyone in your department mark the schedule with planned vacations . . .

2. Dear Mrs. Castle

    Thank you for your order No. 9726. It was shipped on Thursday, March 2. Please let me know if you have not received the merchandise by March 15.

    Sincerely,

    Chris Battel

3. Dear Dr. Caplet

    You are cordially invited to the annual meeting of the fellows of Old Main. We will be celebrating our 100th anniversary this year. Please bring old photos.

    Cordially,

    Sam J. Jones

    SJJ krg

4. Dear Mr. Jacobs

    Subject Order Number 12389 dated 7/6/--

    We have been able to locate only three of the items you ordered. The other two, the special edition of Dickens' A Christmas Carol and the pamphlet on the Constitution, are not available at this time. Please let us know if you want to postpone or cancel the order.

Respectfully,

Jason Sabor

5. Dear Captain Barnes

The oldest record of inspection of the house at 123 South Elm Drive is dated June 14, 1968. Although we have searched for further evidence of insurance coverage prior to that date, we do not have any other older records available. We hope this information is helpful in your investigation of the fire. We are obliged to let Miss Reams, the owner, know of your inquiry.

Sincerely,

Becky Stone

cc Andrea Reams

6.   To   Jason Badder
    From   Samuel Oldcastle
    Date   4/17/--
Subject   New Policy for Travel Requests

Because the budget for corporate travel is limited until the end of the year, all requests must be approved at least ten days in advance. This will allow for proper balancing between territories needing service. Thanks for your cooperation.

7. Dear Ms. Sanchez

You will find that the enclosed information will help you determine which model you would like to order. If we can be of further help, please let us know.

Sincerely,

Keith Hammond

KH jjk

8. Dear Aunt Hilda,

I'm sorry I was late with your birthday gift. Bill was traveling, and the kids kept me busy. We hope to visit on the 3rd of next month. Let me know if that is okay.

Love,

Karen

The answers are in the back of the text-workbook.

EXERCISE 3B
Chapter 3   *COLON*

RULES 1–3

- Insert colons in the following material and write the rule number and letter from the Compact Colon Summary above each colon you insert.
- The uses involve Colon Rules 1, 2, and 3.
- In the last five situations one does not need a colon.

Example: The class will begin at 12:30 p.m.
(1A above the colon)

1. Resolved The Environmental Impact Committee will commission a study of the proposed construction and fund the study from its own resources.

2. The poet read from his latest collection *Rhymes Without Reasons Poems of a Playful Mind.*

3. Mandrake, James R., "The Oldest Veteran," *Historical Journal,* 112 22, August 1993.

4. Bob   Why do you always second guess what I want to say?

   Melanie   You know I don't mean to.

   Bob   Well, it still bothers me, so try to quit.

5. Mr. Chairman, members of the board, and fellow delegates I hope you will forgive the change of agenda. We want to begin this evening with a number of business items and then move on to our featured speaker.

6. Dear Mr. Perez

   We will not be able to attend the convention this year. Although we have found it valuable in the past, the budget this year does not allow travel. We hope to return the following year. I will also notify Bill Johnson, the accommodations coordinator.

   Sincerely,

   Frank Skyler
   cc Bill Johnson

7. The parable of the Good Samaritan is found at Luke 1030–37.

8. Jones, Elmer. *Healthy Nutrition for Everyone.* Philadelphia Nostar Publishing Company, 1993.

9. You will find that a proportion of 5 to 7 is the best for the team and the individual.

10. Dear Ms. Sanger

    Subject Questions on Invoice #5677

    Although your invoice arrived promptly, we have enough questions that we must delay payment until the answers are clear.

Is the first figure in column 3 the total for all items or only for those shipped?

Does the billing for freight include the items shipped under the second delayed delivery?

If you can answer these questions, we can clarify the amount due and get the payment to you.

Sincerely,

Della Jones

pc Allison Walton, Accounts Payable

The answers are in the back of the text-workbook.

INTRODUCE ADDITIONAL CONTENT
Chapter 3   *COLON*

LEARNING OBJECTIVES

After your study of Colon Rule 4, you will be able to:
- Insert colons correctly to introduce additional content.
- Label colon uses to show the type of additional material introduced.

RULE 4: Use colons to INTRODUCE additional content.

A. Lists
- Displayed

- Internal in sentence (Do not separate objects from prepositions or verbs.)

B. Extended quotation
- Displayed

- Internal

C. Extended explanation

D. Amplification for emphasis
E. Additional detail

A.
- Bring the following items:
  – Chips
  – Pretzels
  – Crackers
- You may bring the following supplies for the test: pencils, an eraser, and a ruler.

B.
- Although he was not a gardener,
  Mark Twain noted certain distinctions:
  > I know the taste of the watermelon which has been honestly come by, and I know the taste of the watermelon which has been acquired by art. Both taste good, but the experienced know which tastes best.
- Mark Twain showed his cynic's disdain for telling the truth when he said: "Lying is universal—we *all* do it; we all *must* do it. Therefore, the wise thing is for us diligently to train ourselves to lie thoughtfully . . ."

C. Please let me explain this way:
  the whole is sometimes greater than the sum of its parts.

D. He cared only about one possession: his car.
E. For Sale: mountain cabin
  Note: The test results must be recorded at this time.

Fold out the Compact Colon Summary in the back of the text-workbook so you can see it while you read the explanations and work on the exercises.

F. Connected ideas
- Additional information
- Transitional expressions
  (e.g., i.e., for example, that is)

- Repeated structure

F.
- He toiled all his life: such was his plight.
- Do not use periods with abbreviations for agencies: e.g., FBI, CIA, or DOD. Security guards will provide protection: that is, they will be guarding the door and escorting people to their cars.
- She can be elected: she must be elected.

Fold out the Compact Colon Summary in the back of the text-workbook so you can see it while you read the explanations and work on the exercises.

COLON—INTRODUCTION

The situations using Rule 4 are similar because they all use the colon as an introducer. The colon helps the reader anticipate that additional information will follow. This additional information can be in a number of forms, but the information amplifies the prior statement.

A. Lists

The colon introduces two forms of lists — the displayed list and the internal list.

DISPLAYED LISTS. With the displayed list writers often use the words *follow, following* or *as follows* at the end or near the end of the sentence stem to signal this introduction. The items in the list are highlighted because the lists are set off and surrounded by white space.

Before we attend the meeting, we must assemble the following information:

- Capital projections
- Deadlines
- Regulations

Place the colon immediately after the last word in the sentence stem. The sentence stem without the list is still complete, but the reader would be left with very little concrete information without the list. Sometimes letters or numbers introduce the items in the list. A special symbol such as an asterisk, a dash, or a round, black dot (a *bullet*) may precede each item. Use numbers and letters if the order of the items is important or if you are meeting the style requirements for a particular publication or editor.

Before we attend the meeting, we must assemble the following information:

1. Capital projections
2. Deadlines
3. Regulations

Displayed lists should have parallel forms. Don't mix the forms of words in the lists themselves. Do NOT mix the tense or voice of the verbs.

OTHER PUNCTUATION NOTES. The use of the period with the items in a displayed list puzzles many writers. Here are the general rules.

- You may include periods after letters or numbers introducing the items.
- Do not include periods after the items in a displayed list unless the items themselves are complete sentences.
- Do not include a period only after the last item.

LISTS WITHIN SENTENCES. The second method for using colons with lists is for a colon to introduce lists within a sentence. In this situation the items are separated by commas.

> When you work in the garden you will need the following tools: a hoe, a shovel, a bucket, and elbow grease.

If the items in the list have internal commas, separate the items with a semicolon.

> Please submit the following information: (1) April sales figures, including returns; (2) printing expenses for May; and (3) budget proposal for September, excluding capital items.

These examples could be written as displayed lists. A displayed list generally catches the eye, takes more space, and calls attention to the list itself. As with displayed lists, do not separate phrases. Use parallel structure for the items in the list.

B. Extended quotation

The colon may introduce an extended quotation. In general a comma introduces the direct words of a speaker. However, if the quotation is fairly long and inset from the regular text, then introduce the quotation with a colon.

> Mark Twain traveled extensively. His interest was fueled by his fascination with discovery of places and ideas, which is shown in this passage:
>
> > What is it that confers the noblest delight? What is that which swells a man's breast with pride above that which any other experience can bring to him? Discovery! To know that you are walking where none others have walked; that you are beholding what others may have not seen before; that you are breathing a virgin atmosphere. To give birth to an idea — to discover a great thought.

An extended quotation within a sentence can also be introduced with a colon. The colon introduces a quotation more formally than a comma. A colon introduces a long quotation or one which consists of an independent clause or more than one sentence. By using a colon to introduce a quotation, the writer sets a more formal tone than when using a comma.

> Ms. Valdez said: "We will not accept the compromise plan. It does not offer the required detail to solve the problem, nor does it resolve the budget questions associated with the change in the law. Our position is clear. We must renegotiate."

C. Extended explanation

The extended explanation parallels the extended quotation. In these sentences the writer places a general statement before the colon and then develops the explanation in the clause that follows it.

Please let me explain my point this way: the whole is sometimes greater than the sum of its parts.

The material following the colon explains a general statement or term the writer used in the introductory clause. The term *point* is explained by *the whole is sometimes greater than the sum of its parts.*

The colon shifts the reader's attention to the detailed information which follows it. Make sure that is where you want the reader's attention.

D. Amplification for emphasis

For emphasis the colon can set off a phrase from the main part of a sentence. The colon shifts the emphasis in the sentence to the words which follow the colon.

She was concerned only for her immediate needs: hunger and thirst.

The colon shifts the emphasis and the reader's attention to the words that follow—*hunger and thirst.*
Shifting emphasis is another way to vary your sentences.

E. Additional detail

In some situations the colon separates a general topic from additional detail. Words like *Caution, Note,* and *For Sale* are followed by additional detail and information about what cautions to take, what notes are important, or what items are for sale.

Caution: Close safety cover before starting motor.

Note: Older models will seldom have the replaceable valves.

For Sale: saxophone and clarinet

F. Connected ideas

The colon can play a versatile role in connecting ideas—restatements or amplifications. The colon can connect a phrase or a clause to a sentence where the phrase following the colon relies on the sentence and adds additional information.

phrase   This committee has only one purpose: to evaluate product quality.

clause   The horse will be destroyed if the vet cannot treat the problem: little else can be done.

The colon links sentences that have a similar structure to develop a rhythm and balance. By connecting them with a colon the writer can link the ideas and demonstrate a different emphasis. Often the forms of the sentences that are joined in this way are parallel structures.

She lead the team to victory: she was the only one who could.

In this sentence the subjects are the same. The length of the clauses are about the same. A balance, amplification, and connection make the sentence a more effective one than simply two sentences separated by a period. Using emphasis by connecting with a colon, the writer can show the reader precise meaning.

G. Details with Latin abbreviations and equivalents

Along with some other punctuation marks the colon can introduce the transitional expressions *for example* and *that is* or the abbreviations for their Latin equivalents.

Latin term	Abbreviation	English equivalent
exempli gratia	e.g.	for example
id est	i.e.	that is or namely

You may use a colon to introduce a transitional expression if you want an abrupt break or pause. The colon is more abrupt than a semicolon and weaker than a dash. Parentheses would provide an even more significant break.

> The readers are concerned with the movement of the novel: e.g., the changes in character, the sequence of actions, and the development of tension.

> You will be required to complete the materials before your application is accepted: i.e., you must fill out the form, request approval, and outline the budget.

> Our resources are limited: that is, the budget is only one half of last year's, and we have only 60 percent of the staff.

The English versions are more familiar to most readers. If you use the Latin forms, use colons correctly.

SUMMARY

The colon uses in Rule 4 are varied. The colon may connect parts of a sentence or introduce additional material. This material may be lists of single words or long phrases and clauses. It may be quotations or explanations. The material may be additional detail to emphasize or to connect additional ideas in clauses or phrases. Related ideas connected by the colon or introduced by transitional expressions need colons. The colon shifts the reader's attention to the information which follows it.

In the first three colon rules, the colon connects with a variety of mechanical and familiar uses such as indicating time, following salutations in business letters, and separating parts of titles. The colon is surpassed only by the comma in versatility and diversity of uses, yet it is used far less frequently.

EXERCISE 4A
Chapter 3 *COLON*

RULE 4

- Insert colons in the following sentences and write the rule number and letter from the Compact Colon Summary above each colon you insert.
- All the uses involve Rule 4.
- In the last five situations one does not need a colon.

Example: My goal is a simple one*4D*: measurable results.

1. We will need the following to begin the cleanup project

     - Volunteers
     - Transportation
     - Permits

2. You will find that I don't care about written plans your evaluation depends on results.

3. We never fool ourselves we only try to fool others.

4. Please add the following to your list of concerns

     - Adequate budget
     - Sufficient resources
     - Clearly defined schedule

5. Note the completed reports will be available after the first of the week.

6. In all of his former positions he cared primarily about his bosses' concerns profits.

7. We will find that the main point can be summarized in Martin's latest remark

     The golden age of the large corporation is behind us. From now on we will see the emergence of the smaller, more responsive organization.

8. As we finish the environmental project, be sure to complete the following tests air quality, water quality, and noise impact.

9. She felt that this was the main problem in providing an adequate solution to the problem all of the major opponents had different alternatives upon which they could not agree.

10. The final implementation will take several months because the details will not be completed as quickly as we originally planned.

The answers are in the back of the text-workbook.

EXERCISE 4B
Chapter 3   *COLON*

RULES 1–4

- Insert colons in the following material and write the rule number and letter from the Compact Colon Summary above each colon you insert.
- The uses involve all colon rules.
- In the last five situations one does not need a colon.

Example: My goal is a simple one **4D**: measurable results.

1. The minister lead the service with a passage from James 4 12–15.

2. Our proposal will need to meet all of the requirements sufficient staff, adequate manufacturing facilities, and adequate transportation alternatives.

3. For the party we will have to arrange for the following

   - Entertainment
   - Food
   - Doorprizes

4. As the planned changes take effect, we will notice the following

   - Improved customer relations
   - Better profit margins
   - More productive employees

5. The plane will be departing from Gate 17 at 645 a.m.

6. Dear Dr. Marshall

   The information you requested is included in the reprints I have
   enclosed. I hope you find them valuable. If I can be of further service,
   please call us at 1-800-555-3456.

   Sincerely,

   Carl Wohl

7. Caution the cover plate must be secured before starting the unit or electric shock may occur.

8. Please note that the following items are required for our new customer's kit

   - Additional order forms
   - Warranty registration
   - Service center telephone numbers

9.
```
     To    Cassie Lowery
   From    Carl Faberg
   Date    3/3/--
Subject    Next year's budget request
```
Be sure to send the figures to me by Friday. In addition, we will . . .

10. Maybe I can finish this soon there are more ways than one to solve a problem.

11. Mr. Chairman, Madame President, and members of the board as you can imagine I am highly honored to receive this award. Your interest in my work has been a personally satisfying return for the effort.

12. Ester   We will have to make the best of the situation.

    Tom   I know, but you'll have to help me.

13. In summary, the new staff will be faced with several problems such as low worker morale, tight budgets, and a significant backlog of work.

14. The last thing the author wrote was the title of the book which was *Personal Growth How to Change Your Habits*.

15. The biggest problem facing the new manager was that the return rate exceeded the sales rate by a ratio of 32.

The answers are in the back of the text-workbook.

APOSTROPHE

Chapter 4   Small but often misunderstood

Often little things trouble us most. Except for the comma, the apostrophe is perhaps the most often misused punctuation mark. The apostrophe's primary purpose shows minor adjustments in word form. Confusion may be caused by the reasons for the change in form. In one situation the apostrophe can show a plural while in another situation it may mean possession. Although most punctuation marks are sentence-level marks (separating parts, showing relationships, or making connections), the apostrophe is a word-level punctuation mark. Look at it as a spelling tool rather than a sentence tool. Three rules govern the apostrophe. Rule 1 deals with possessives, Rule 2 deals with deletion, and Rule 3 deals with plurals.

POSSESSION
Chapter 4   *APOSTROPHE*

LEARNING OBJECTIVES

After your study of Apostrophe Rule 1, you will be able to:
- Insert apostrophes correctly to show possession.
- Label apostrophe uses to indicate whether possession is singular or plural.

RULE 1: Use apostrophes to indicate POSSESSION.

A. Singular words
B. Plural words

"Plus" Diagram

	Singular	**Plural**
Regular	boy	boys
Possessive	boy's	boys'

Fold out the Compact Apostrophe Summary in the back of the text-workbook so you can see it while you read the explanations and work on the exercises.

APOSTROPHE—POSSESSION

In Rule 1 (the most frequently used rule) an apostrophe shows possessive form or ownership. First, consider this simple example.

the boy's hat

While the word *boy* is a noun, in this phrase *boy's* is an adjective showing the hat belongs to the boy.

Although this is easy to see when written, writers sometimes have trouble because when spoken this use sounds the same as the forms we use for other situations. Many writers have confused the method for showing plural (a number greater than one) with the method for showing possession (ownership). Both situations add an *s* with or without other letters and marks to show these two different meanings.

SPELLING PLURALS—A BRIEF DETOUR. Make the plural form of a word by adding an *s* to the end of it. This method is used for many of the nouns in our language. Words where this is not true are usually words borrowed from other languages.

Singular	Plural
boy	boys
girl	girls

If a word ends in *s* or a sound that is similar to *s* such as *z, sh,* or *ch,* the plural is different. Because it is too difficult to pronounce the *s* added right after another *s*-type sound, we insert a vowel between the sounds.

Singular	Plural
boss	bosses
church	churches

For words that end in *y,* the plural is formed in yet another way with two variations. When we make the plural form of a word ending in the letter *y* following a consonant, we change the *y* to *i* and add *es.*

Singular	Plural
baby	babies
family	families

If the word ends in *y* following a vowel, we leave the *y* and just add s.

Singular	Plural
tray	trays
monkey	monkeys

Some words change internally to form a plural like *woman* which becomes *women.* Other words like *deer* are both singular and plural depending upon the situation in which they are used. These words are exceptions to the basic rules. Here are those basic rules in a chart which may be easier to remember. (See Figure 4-1.)

FIGURE 4-1
Plural forms

PLURAL FORMS

BASE WORD	TO FORM PLURAL	EXAMPLES Singular	Plural
regular	add *s*	hat	hats
ends with an *s*-type sound	add *es*	church	churches
ends with a consonant + *y*	change *y* to *i* and add *es*	family	families
ends with a vowel + *y*	add *s*	day	days

RETURN TO RULE 1

Now look at Apostrophe Rule 1. Draw a "Plus" Diagram (a large plus sign) or look at the diagram. Across the top put the words *singular* and *plural*. On the left side put *regular* on top and *possessive* on the bottom. Now fill in the chart to show all four different meanings of a given word.

"Plus" Diagram

	Singular	Plural
Regular		
Possessive		

A. Singular words   The upper left square is a regular singular form. The lower left square has the form from the upper left with the apostrophe and *s* added to show possession by the singular form.

B. Plural words   The regular plural form that goes in the upper right square is the one where you just add *s* or *es* to the regular singular form. In the lower right corner ownership of more than one boy is shown by adding an apostrophe after the *s* in the plural form, *boys*. For example, if several boys had a club, it would belong to all of them. It would then be the *boys'* club. Here is the "plus" diagram completed with the word *boy* and its forms.

	Singular	**Plural**
Regular	boy	boys
Possessive	boy's	boys'

All but the one in the upper left sound the same. Although they sound the same, they must be written differently. Four distinct meanings are needed.

	Singular	**Plural**
Regular	boss	bosses
Possessive	boss's	bosses'

Every word has four forms to show the four distinct meanings.

IRREGULAR FORMS

Some words do not follow the pattern of simply adding *s* or *es*. Sometimes the odd combination of sounds force us to spell the plural of a word in another way. One notable example is the word *woman*.

	Singular	**Plural**
Regular	woman	women
Possessive	woman's	women's

The apostrophe does not follow the *s* in the plural possessive form because the word changes to plural internally. Some other examples are *child* and *man*.

THE *S* PROBLEM

Since we have a difficult time pronouncing words which end in *s* and then add *s* to make the possessive, we have generally accepted the written possessive form with only the apostrophe added. Even though this does not fit with the general rule, we accept it.

	Singular	**Plural**
Regular	hostess	hostesses
Possessive	hostess's	hostesses'

	Singular	**Plural**
Regular	James	Jameses
Possessive	James's or James'	Jameses'

SOME ODDITIES

One unique application of this rule occurs with special words such as *conscience*. This word does not end in *s*, but the *c* sounds like *s*. When you build a possessive form of this word, then you need to handle it as if it were an *s*. For example:

I hope you are right for your conscience' sake.

It follows the logic of words ending with an *s*-sound even though it does not end with the letter *s* itself.

Compound or hypenated forms of words may also be unique. When you write words connected with *and* to make a compound, only apply the apostrophe to form the possessive of the second word.

We saw a replica of Wilbur and Orville's plane when we visited the Air and Space Museum.

The plane was jointly owned, but the apostrophe and *s* are added only to the second word.

The same rule applies when the combination is achieved through hyphenation. Use the possessive with the last part of the compound word only.

The managers will listen to the rank-and-file's request.

Finally, certain expressions use an apostrophe for the sake of form even though the logic of pure possession is flawed. Some writers call these false possessives. Many of these words express amounts of time or money.

a dollar's worth of candy
a day's pay
two months' time
three weeks' work

The dollar does not really own the candy, and the day does not own the pay. However, in many such commonly used expressions, the possessive form is accepted as a correct usage.

USAGE NOTE. Some special words such as company names and product names that are officially spelled with or without apostrophes should be spelled as their owners dictate even if they break the rules.

SUMMARY

The "plus" diagram will clarify most of the apostrophe use for you. Think about which meaning you really need. Do you mean something owned by more than one, or do you simply refer to more than one?

EXERCISE 1   **RULE 1**
Chapter 4   *APOSTROPHE*

- Complete a "plus" diagram to show singular, plural, singular possessive, and plural possessives of words.
- Insert apostrophes in the following sentences and write the rule number and letter from the Compact Apostrophe Summary above each apostrophe you insert.
- All the uses involve Rule 1.
- In the last five sentences one does not need an apostrophe.

Example: The player *1A*'s concerns were known when he argued with the coach.

Complete a "plus" diagram for the each of the following words:

1. church

2. aunt

3. job

4. The films title reflected the directors thinking. It was *All My Trials*.

5. The runners best effort was not enough to win the race.

6. My report will not meet the bosss expectations.

7. The twins will need more attention. Now the babies needs are met by two people.

8. The varying notches will make the keys comparison difficult.

9. The keeper asked, "How will we remodel the monkeys cage? We have no place for them."

10. The womens organization will meet more regularly after their organizational meetings are complete.

11. Yesterdays results will be reported in tomorrows newspaper.

12. I doubt his conscience will let him forget.

13. We will not be able to finish the project on time even with the three weeks study we have devoted.

14. The shopper asked the clerk for directions to the childrens department.

15. The police investigated the robbery at Jones Garage.

The answers are in the back of the text-workbook.

DELETION
Chapter 4   *APOSTROPHE*

LEARNING OBJECTIVES

After your study of Apostrophe Rule 2, you will be able to:
- Insert apostrophes correctly as deletions in contracted forms.
- Label apostrophe uses to indicate which type of shortened form is used.

RULE 2: Use apostrophes to indicate DELETION (contraction forms).

A. Numbers	A. '76 (1976)
B. Letters	B. can't (cannot)
	doesn't (does not)
	nat'l (national)
C. In dialogue to show pronunciation	C. "Well, if you are goin', then I am too."
D. Certain invented expressions	D. The supervisor ok'd the order.

Fold out the Compact Apostrophe Summary in the back of the text-workbook so you can see it while you read the explanations and work on the exercises.

APOSTROPHE—DELETION

The second apostrophe rule shows that minor portions of words or phrases have been left out.

A. Numbers

When you refer to dates, the year is sometimes shortened by leaving off the *19* before the specific year within the century.

> I remember back in '67 when we had a winning season.

The apostrophe simply provides a shorter way of writing a year. Do not use it when you are writing the month and day along with the year. When the date is that specific, use the complete form.

> I remember when that tradition began on May 14, 1977.

If you are using a form of a date with slashes or dashes, avoid the apostrophe.

Use	5/6/93	Not	5/6/'93
Use	10-21-88	Not	10-21-'88

B. Letters

Apostrophes show where certain letters are left out of words with shortened or contracted forms. Although these forms are not always considered proper in formal work, they are frequently used in routine writing. The most common deletion is the *o* in *not* when combined with a verb.

does not	doesn't
should not	shouldn't
cannot	can't

Another common contraction is a pronoun plus *have, will,* or *are.*

I have	I've
I will	I'll

you have	you've
you will	you'll
you are	you're

they have	they've
they will	they'll
they are	they're

The apostrophe can substitute for a combination of letters. The contracted form of *national—nat'l—*is one example. Contractions do not have periods after them as abbreviations do.

The apostrophe can also show a contraction between a noun and the verb *is.* For example, you could write this sentence two ways.

> The speaker is going to discuss the issues.
> The speaker's going to discuss the issues.

Don't be confused between the use of the apostrophe in a possessive and in a contraction.

The speaker's name was listed on the program.
The speaker's going to explain the history of the region.

Both of these situations use *speaker's,* but they are different uses. The first is a possessive — the name belongs to the speaker. The second is a contraction of *speaker* and *is.*

C. Dialogue

When writers show variations of speech in dialogue, they use the apostrophe to show deletions. Some writers such as Mark Twain are masters at communicating regional speech variations with adjusted spelling and the apostrophe. The apostrophe can hint at the way our natural speech drops letter sounds.

"I'm not willin' to help you with it."

"I don't wanna, an' I don't care what you think."

"They said 'twas everythin' they wanted."

D. Invented expressions

Sometimes writers use apostrophes to invent expressions that are variations of words. The common one that is in the Compact Apostrophe Summary is *ok'd.*

These expressions also come from abbreviations. The abbreviation for a noun is sometimes used as a past tense verb and then the apostrophe is applied to show the deletion of the *e.* For example, in boxing the noun *knock out* is abbreviated *KO.*

Martinez KO'd Smith in the fourth round.

"The investigator ID'd the suspect and made the arrest."

SUMMARY

The apostrophe can show that some numbers or letters are omitted. Examples of omissions include the century portion of the year, letters in contracted word forms, and parts of words that reflect regional or slang speech. Certain invented expressions also use apostrophes.

EXERCISE 2A
RULE 2
Chapter 4   *APOSTROPHE*

- Insert apostrophes in the following sentences and write the rule number and letter from the Compact Apostrophe Summary above each apostrophe you insert.
- All the uses involve Rule 2.
- In the last five sentences one does not need an apostrophe.

Example: I remember back in ²ᴬ '88 when that was not a problem.

1. We cant seem to find all of the books youve ordered.

2. "If you insist, well start doin it your way."

3. Why wont she listen to my ideas?

4. The champion KOd the challenger in the third round.

5. The guards will find that the monitor isnt in its old location.

6. Ill take care of the telephone order if youll finish the log book.

7. We cant complete your order until you give us all of the instructions.

8. We may find that although the manager okd the request, it was not completed correctly.

9. "If youre not ready, we may be startin without you."

10. Her note read, "Cancel the natl meeting."

11. "Thatll cost us even if we can get past the initial problem."

12. Maybe the older of the dogs will teach the younger one by example.

13. I remember that we had a much better team in 88 than in 89.

14. The coldest weather will cause the most damage to the crop; dont you agree?

15. The experienced editors will complete the manuscript even though they wont have all the final artwork for another month.

The answers are in the back of the text-workbook.

EXERCISE 2B

RULES 1–2

Chapter 4 *APOSTROPHE*

- Complete a "plus" diagram to show singular, plural, singular possessive, and plural possessives of words.
- Insert apostrophes in the following sentences and write the rule number and letter from the Compact Apostrophe Summary above each apostrophe you insert.
- The uses involve Rules 1 and 2.
- In the last five sentences one does not need an apostrophe.

Example: You′re the only one who can handle the task.
2B

1. All instructors should attend at least one leaders conference.

2. "We cant find all of the answers. Are you goin to help?"

3. Complete a "plus" diagram for the following word: fox

4. How can we observe those pigeons nesting activities?

5. The oldest characters in the play will have to have two weeks growth of beard.

6. "Samuel, I know we filed the application forms in 88."

7. Complete a "plus" diagram for the following word: child

8. "Has the boss okd the purchase order yet?"

9. "Im sure your leavin will hurt his feelings."

10. The waiters will be serving the desert after the speakers message.

11. The plan for a pilot project must be scrapped because the budget will be too small for the groups needs.

12. Shell have to make all the arrangements on her own.

13. "If you say it is important, then we will have to consider it our teams best chance at the championship."

14. The players will be given special passes before the games.

15. The heiress inheritance was far more than she had expected.

The answers are in the back of the text-workbook.

RULE 3

PLURALS
Chapter 4   *APOSTROPHE*

LEARNING OBJECTIVES

After your study of Apostrophe Rule 3, you will be able to:
- Insert apostrophes correctly as plural forms.
- Label apostrophe uses to indicate the which type of plural form is used.

RULE 3: Use apostrophes for PLURALS of symbols and abbreviations.

A. Characters
   (letters, numbers, or symbols)

B. Words referred to as words
C. Abbreviations
   (without apostrophe also accepted when
    abbreviation is all capital letters)

A. a's   3's
   t's   &'s   i's
   I am looking for your size 5's.
B. In your speech you used too many *and's.*
C. CPU's (CPUs)
   MPI's (MPIs)

Fold out the Compact Apostrophe Summary in the back of the text-workbook so you can see it while you read the explanations and work on the exercises.

APOSTROPHE—PLURALS

A. Plurals of characters

Apostrophes can show plurals of characters—letters, numbers, or symbols. An apostrophe separates the *s* at the end of the plural form from the character. Without an apostrophe the meaning may be confusing.

> Be sure to dot your *i*'s.

The writer means more than one letter *i*. If the apostrophe was left out, the form would look like the word *is*.

This rule with the plural of characters applies to letters, numbers, and other symbols such as the ampersand (&).

> The 3's on this computer printout are not clear.
> Do not use #'s in your formal writing.

B. Words referred to as words

Sometimes we need to point out a word in writing. The plural uses an apostrophe and an *s*.

> Why did you capitalize all of the *or*'s?

The apostrophe used in combination with the *s* shows that the word is plural, but the word does not carry its usual meaning. The word is spoken about or referred to.

C. Abbreviations

As with some other uses of language and grammar, apostrophe usage with abbreviations is in transition. Some authorities say the apostrophe is not necessary; others say it is. During a transitional period like this, you will see it used both ways. Over time the new method will emerge, and the old one will fade. Be consistent in one piece of writing.

> The computer is controlled by a CPU (central processing unit). Most CPU's are designed for certain kinds of data.

You could also correctly write the word without the apostrophe .

> The computer is controlled by a CPU (central processing unit). Most CPUs are designed for certain kinds of data.

USAGE NOTE. An apostrophe should not be used in possessive pronouns like *theirs, ours, yours,* or *its*. This confusion occurs particularly with *it's* and *its*. The word with the apostrophe—*it's*—is the contracted form of *it is*. The *its* form is a pronoun like *yours* or *ours*. It does not use an apostrophe.

SUMMARY

Do not overgeneralize this rule. Use apostrophes to avoid confusion in spelling. Although the apostrophe is used for plurals, these plurals are special. Use it only to show plurals of characters, abbreviations, and words used as objects. Otherwise, the general rules of making plurals hold true.

EXERCISE 3A
Chapter 4   *APOSTROPHE*

RULE 3

> ● Insert the apostrophes in the following sentences where they are needed and write the rule number and letter from the Compact Apostrophe Summary above each apostrophe you insert.
> ● All of the uses involve Rule 3.

Example: Watch out. In this manuscript some of the i 's look like 1 's.

1.   You cannot always tell ts from +s.

2.   You have used connective ands too many times in your essay.

3.   Be sure that your letter contains enough yous.

4.   I am looking for your loafers; where are your size 8s?

5.   The CPUs will be turned off for maintenance after midnight.

6.   As the CRTs were turned on, the message let everyone know there would be problems all day.

7.   The champion will earn As on the evaluations.

8.   The older PDRs can be stacked at the end of the lot.

9.   The computer printouts made the difference between 3s and 8s difficult to see.

10.   The poker player could not decide whether to keep the 10s or 2s.

The answers are in the back of the text-workbook.

EXERCISE 3B
Chapter 4   *APOSTROPHE*
RULES 1–3

- **Insert the apostrophes in the following sentences where they are needed and write the rule number and letter from the Compact Apostrophe Summary above each apostrophe you insert.**
- **The uses involve all apostrophe rules.**
- **In the last five sentences one does not need an apostrophe.**

Example: The welds will be used in all the structure's main joints. _(1A)_

1. As you review these papers, check for missing ts at the end of sentences.

2. The consumer price index (CPI) is frequently revised, but the CPIs do not change all the other indicators.

3. The letters must be completed by the end of todays shift.

4. You have used too many pauses and uhs in your sales presentation.

5. Additional firefighters were needed to battle the fires forward movement.

6. Three additional CTIs will be needed to complete the assembly of the Model 331.

7. Make the title tell a story. Use it to grab a readers attention.

8. "Excuse me, can you guide me to the rack with size 34s?"

9. Theyll all fit if we rearrange them according to size instead of color.

10. Any more ORUs we need will require additional modification.

11. I hope his conscience doesnt bother him tomorrow.

12. We cannot accept any more trade-ins of last years model.

13. Patents will be issued for all of the inventors inventions even though he will not be selling them to a manufacturer.

14. James leadership makes the group work together well as a team.

15. The patience of all of the employees will be needed for the new plan to work.

The answers are in the back of the text-workbook.

QUOTATION MARKS

Chapter 5   Who said that?

Quotation marks enclose the titles of some artistic or literary works, show unusual or special use of words, and indicate the exact words of a speaker. Use quotation marks to highlight these items. Your readers expect to see quotation marks in the right places. Be sure to control your writing by using the rules outlined on the Compact Quotation Mark Summary.

TITLES

Chapter 5   *QUOTATION MARKS*

LEARNING OBJECTIVES

After your study of Quotation Mark Rule 1, you will be able to:
- Insert quotation marks correctly to show titles.
- Label quotation mark uses to show the titles of a chapter, article, song, or program.

RULE 1: Use quotation marks to show TITLES for some artistic works (others use italics/underline).

A. Chapter

B. Article

C. Song

D. Radio and TV programs

A. After reading the introduction, you should read "Chapter 3: The Golden Basket."

B. The lead article for the evening edition was "Governors Decide Funding."

C. Jason B's latest hit is "My Love, You're Special."

D. Will you watch "Sports Headlines" tonight?

Fold out the Compact Quotation Mark Summary in the back of the text-workbook so you can see it while you read the explanations and work on the exercises.

QUOTATION MARKS—TITLES

Quotation marks highlight or call attention by enclosing the titles of some short creative works. This use includes the titles of parts of complete published works such as chapters in a book or articles in a magazine or journal. The titles of books and magazines should appear in italics. If you do not have italic type available, then underline these titles.

This simple rule will help you remember when to use quotation marks with titles. The short works get the short little marks. The long works get the long mark — the underline. Titles of short works such as song titles, titles of radio and TV programs, and works such as article titles and chapter titles are enclosed in quotation marks.

A. Chapter

"The Game Begins" is the longest chapter in the book.

B. Article

"Help for the Helpless" appeared in the last issue of your magazine.

C. Song

My favorite song last year was "My Love is Lonely."

D. Radio and TV programs

He began his career as an announcer on "NewsWatch" on KMMT.

SUMMARY

Use quotation marks to enclose the titles of songs, radio and TV programs, and short works that are part of a complete published work such as chapters in a book or articles in a magazine.

EXERCISE 1
Chapter 5   *QUOTATION MARKS*

RULE 1

- Insert quotation marks in the following sentences and write the rule number and letter from the Compact Quotation Mark Summary above each quotation mark you insert.
- All the uses involve Rule 1.
- In the last five sentences one does not need quotation marks.

Example: The name of the article in the *Harpers* was ^1B "What is Our Policy in Central America?" 1B

1. We will probably sing Auld Lang Syne again this New Year's Eve.

2. After she published her book, Emma appeared on The Bill Morgan Show to answer questions.

3. The assignment covered the last chapter, Causes of the War.

4. The authors needed more information for their article on baseball — Greats of the 50's.

5. Of all his hits the one I liked best was Baby, I Love You.

6. The morning program on WBGA is Wake Up With Wanda.

7. His recent publications included two articles, New Issues in Economic Policy and Global Economic Change Creates Opportunity.

8. When she finishes the editing, her new book, *Help for the Hassled,* will be ready for publication.

9. The radio announcer began the series with two new songs, He's in Love and Summer Beat.

10. The most quoted chapter in Dr. Martinez' new book is Chapter 4, Finding Your Place.

The answers are in the back of the text-workbook.

WORDS USED IN A SPECIAL SENSE
Chapter 5   *QUOTATION MARKS*

LEARNING OBJECTIVES

After your study of Quotation Mark Rule 2, you will be able to:
- Insert quotation marks correctly to show words used in a special sense.
- Label the quotation mark uses to show how the words are used in a special sense.

RULE 2: Use quotation marks to show a WORD used in a special sense.

A. Intentional misspelling
   or use of poor grammar

B. Used with special expression
   such as *signed, labeled,* or *marked*

C. Technical or slang terms

D. Refer to the word itself
   (underline or italics is preferred,
   but quotation marks are also used)

A. I know you don't "wanna."

B. The letter was signed "Martin Cuzos."

C. The "rotary sleeve" clutch was used on the
   new model.
   No matter how we ask Bill, he "ain't workin'
   with ya."

D. Delete "often" in the second sentence.

Fold out the Compact Quotation Mark Summary in the back of the text-workbook so you can see it while you read the explanations and work on the exercises.

QUOTATION MARKS—SPECIAL USAGE

Quotation marks often identify words used in a special or unusual way.

A. Intentional misspellings or poor grammar

Sometimes you will need to show intentional misspelling or incorrect grammar. To show these uses you can enclose the problem words in quotation marks to highlight their special use.

> Although she said "supposubly," everyone knew what she meant.

> You don't "gotta" do anything.

Let your reader know that you are aware of incorrect spelling usage by enclosing those uses in quotation marks.

B. Special expressions

You may need to refer specifically to certain phrases or special spellings of other information. These references are signaled by such words as *signed, labeled,* and *marked.* Following the signal word you should enclose the specific information in quotation marks.

> He signed the letter "Master William Smith."

> The outer package was labeled "Fragile"; the inner package was labeled "Very Fragile."

C. Technical or slang terms

You may find it necessary to show the special use of slang or technical terms. If, however, for a technical term your audience would know the term, you need not use quotation marks.

> We will be demonstrating the new "inverse ratio" gearing later.

> You can recognize the use of "cool" when it does not mean slightly cold.

As you use these special terms, highlight them when they do not match the degree of technical speciality or formality in the rest of the text. If you overuse this technique, the highlighting will lose its effectiveness.

D. The word itself

Use Rule 2D where quotation marks refer to a word itself rather than the word's meaning. Not all style guides agree on this rule. Many style guides prefer italics or underlining for this purpose.

> As you write your response, be sure to write "preferred" clearly.

Unless you are using a style guide that requires you to use quotation marks for this purpose, use underlining or italics instead.

SUMMARY

Words in a special sense can be enclosed in quotation marks. You may use quotation marks to show intentional misspellings or poor grammar. Use quotation marks after a special signal expression such as *signed* or *marked* to indicate specific information. You can also use quotation marks to enclose technical terms within nontechnical material. Show slang terms the same way. Quotation marks can show a reference to the word itself but this is not the preferred use.

EXERCISE 2A

RULE 2

Chapter 5   *QUOTATION MARKS*

- Insert quotation marks in the following examples and write the rule number and letter from the Compact Quotation Mark Summary above each quotation mark you insert.
- All the uses involve Rule 2.
- In the last five sentences one does not need quotation marks.

Example: You eliminate contractions like $\overset{2D}{“}$ can't $\overset{2D}{”}$ and $\overset{2D}{“}$ won't $\overset{2D}{”}$ from your formal writing.

1. I have heard him pronounce the word caterlog.

2. The word read can be present tense or past tense depending on its context.

3. The boxes were labeled both flammable and inflammable; no wonder it confused people.

4. The computer programmer answered that the problem was caused by an unresolved circular memory access within the program.

5. Check closely to see that all the homonyms like sale and sail are correctly used in your writing.

6. Fortunately the clerk had marked the receipt paid so there was no question about the payment.

7. Even though Mark did not know what she meant, the technician explained that the problem was an extended condenser reaction to the weather.

8. Dr. Martinez had initialed the chart DVM, and the new nurse misunderstood.

9. We should not answer all the questions with other questions.

10. Brenda could not think of a reply except that she really didn't wanna help with the decorating.

The answers are in the back of the text-workbook.

EXERCISE 2B   RULES 1–2
Chapter 5   *QUOTATION MARKS*

- Insert quotation marks in the following examples and write the rule number and letter from the Compact Quotation Mark Summary above each quotation mark you insert.
- The uses involve Rules 1 and 2.
- In the last five sentences one does not need quotation marks.

Example: Sam completed his article, ᴵᴮ "New Players Add Strength," ᴵᴮ just before the deadline.

1. We will be able to sing both Auld Lang Syne and Holiday Cheer in the concert.

2. As you write the response letters, be sure not to use any long words like anticipatory or cogitations; use simpler words like planning and thoughts.

3. Helena Plumb blasted the planning commission for a new sports franchise in her column, No Hope for the Impossible, which was in yesterday's paper.

4. You will see a major contrast between Ted's character in an early chapter like Chapter 2, Which Way? and the later chapters like Chapter 17, Division of Labor.

5. Linguists, those who study languages scientifically, follow the patterns of words common in several languages like the words for mother, father, or uncle.

6. The doctor told the family that vertebral osteoporosis caused their grandmother's pain.

7. When she joined station WGGM, Wilma Buckman became the producer of Late Night Life.

8. Dear Mrs. Smiley:

   We cannot accept your article, Tough Times on Wall Street, at this time because our next issues are already planned. We wish you luck submitting it elsewhere.

9. The program manager at the radio station would not allow the announcers to play songs such as Friendly Faces or Old Patterns because they did not fit with the new programming approach.

10. Like most authors, you can break the writing of a book into chapters to organize the work.

11. They changed the evening news program from News Day Review to City Watch because the market researchers said the sample audience liked it better.

12. Josie insisted she seen the entire incident, but no one believed her.

13. Frank Smaller wrote both the words and music to his hit Run Far—Run Fast.

14. The secretary labeled the envelope first class so there would be no doubt about its status.

15. The February issue of *Spelunkers' Digest* carried an article, Big Holes—Little Holes, about recent cave discoveries.

The answers are in the back of the text-workbook.

DIRECT WORDS OF A SPEAKER
Chapter 5   *QUOTATION MARKS*

LEARNING OBJECTIVES

After your study of Quotation Mark Rule 3, you will be able to:
- Insert quotation marks correctly with the direct words of a speaker.
- Label quotation mark uses to show whether the quotation is within a sentence, within another quotation, or a long quotation.

RULE 3: Use quotation marks to show the DIRECT WORDS of a speaker.

A. Within a sentence

A. Bill said, "I want to finish the report."
   "This meeting will now come to order," the director announced.
   "Marie," her friend said, "you must finish this project."

B. Within another quotation

B. Tom said, "Joe's comment was simply, 'Ugh.' "

C. Long quotations
   • Within text

C.
   • The speaker closed with these remarks: "The future of this organization is in your hands. We can grow and prosper or languish. The choice is yours." The speaker received a standing ovation.
   • Phyllis showed her feelings when she replied in this way:
   "We will not care about the new report until it is complete. Yet you may express my concern to all of the other staff members. No excuses will be allowed."

   • Blocked off
   (acceptable but not preferred.)

Fold out the Compact Quotation Mark Summary in the back of the text-workbook so you can see it while you read the explanations and work on the exercises.

QUOTATION MARKS—SPEAKER'S WORDS

When you write someone else's exact words, you must show that the words are not yours. You can use various combinations of explanations and direct quotes in your writing. In general, three situations involve a speaker's direct words: (1) quotations within sentences, (2) quotations within another quotation, and (3) long quotations which include sentences of their own.

A. Within a sentence

The most frequent need for quotation marks is to separate the direct words of a speaker from the descriptions the author uses to color the situation where the words were spoken. In the sentence the descriptive words may come before or after the direct words. Notice that the description can introduce, follow, or interrupt the speaker's exact words.

> Maria said, "We will attend the meeting if we arrive in time."

> "We will attend the meeting if we arrive in time," Maria said.

> "We will attend the meeting," Maria said, "if we arrive in time."

The words *Maria said* interrupted the last quotation. The quotation marks surround only the direct words of the speaker, and commas separate the quoted text from the description.

B. Within another quotation

When someone is quoted within another person's direct words, use single quotation marks within the double quotation marks to identify the quote within a quote.

> Betty complained as she carried the dishes to the kitchen, "I never get any help. Garfield always says 'It's not my job to help.'"

The single marks are used like the double marks. Notice that the period ending the quote within a quote is inside the single marks which are inside the double marks. This means that the sentence ends with a second single mark closing the internal quote within a quote and the second double mark closing the entire quote. The same rule with single quotation marks holds true when the reason is one of the other rules such as a title.

> Michi replied, "I really did want to read the article, 'Help for Holiday Dieting.'"

C. Long quotations

Quoted paragraphs or other long quotes are treated differently. The preferred method for a long quote is to separate it from the main text and give it special margins. This is called a *blocked* or *set off quotation.* Since it is set off, quotation marks are not needed. If the quotation is longer than a sentence, and it *is* written within the normal text, then enclose the quotation within quotation marks. Insert the quotation marks at the start and end of the quotation. Do not use a separate set of marks with each sentence. If the quotation *is not* written within the text and will take several lines, you should block it or set it off *without quotation marks*. Although style guides and editors differ, segments longer than four to six lines should be set off.

- Quotation within text:

    Although Betsy was tired, she continued her speech: "Later this evening we will be inspired to improve sales. I want that inspiration to last longer than just this evening. What can we do to make it last until our next meeting?"

- Blocked or set off quotation:

    Although Betsy was tired, she continued her speech:

    > Later this evening we will be inspired to improve sales. I want that inspiration to last longer than just this evening. What can we do to make it last until our next meeting?

Another method that some publications use shows quoted paragraphs by using opening quotation marks at the beginning of every quoted paragraph but closing quotation marks only at the end of the last paragraph. This material is not set off from the other text. It uses the same margins as the normal text that surrounds it. When several paragraphs are quoted, the quotation marks begin the quotation and are used at the beginning of each consecutive quoted paragraph.

> When we finished the building project, the manager gathered us together for his final remarks.
>
> "I want to thank all of you for your efforts. We have been able to finish the project one day ahead of schedule. That was only possible because you all worked together as a team. Thanks.
>
> "In addition, I would like to announce that the next project will begin on Tuesday after we have all had an opportunity to relax over the weekend. The bonus will be determined after we calculate the final costs and profit margin. Again, thank you all."

Notice that the first paragraph does not end in a quotation mark. The second paragraph begins with a quotation mark, and then the whole quotation ends with quotation mark.

USAGE NOTES. Some confusion exists for many writers about using quotation marks with commas and other punctuation. The Compact Quotation Mark Summary has some reminders at the bottom. Place commas and periods inside the quotation marks. Place semicolons and colons outside the quotation marks. Exclamation and question marks can be placed inside or outside the quotation marks depending upon the situation.

Does the question or exclamation mark apply to the entire sentence or only to the quotation? If the direct words of the speaker were said as a question, then the question mark goes inside the quotation marks. If the writer is asking a question that includes the direct words of a speaker, then the question mark goes outside the quotation marks. Similar reasoning applies to the exclamation mark.

Lois finally asked the magic question, "When will it be my turn?"

The witness calmly reported that Maurice had shouted "Surprise!"

Will we ever understand Tom's comment, "The fear is only within us"?

Mrs. Ferguson said, "No school tomorrow"!

In the last two sentences the writer is asking a question or making an exclamation. The question mark or exclamation mark is placed outside the quotation marks.

Dashes may also be placed either inside or outside the quotation marks depending upon the situation. If the thought being quoted breaks off, place the dash inside the quotation marks.

Mrs. Sutton said, "What in the world—"

Place the dash outside closing quotation marks if the sentence that contains the quote breaks off.

If I have to listen once more to "Sing To The World"—

SUMMARY

Quotation marks highlight words according to rules that the reader expects. Use them to highlight the direct words of a speaker. Use them with caution to highlight the special use of a word. Use quotation marks to surround the titles of some artistic works.

EXERCISE 3A   RULE 3
Chapter 5   *QUOTATION MARKS*

- Insert quotation marks in the following examples and write the rule number and letter from the Compact Quotation Mark Summary above each quotation mark you insert.
- All the uses involve Rule 3.
- In the last five sentences one does not need quotation marks.

Example: Jamie showed that she was too tired to finish when she said, *3A* "My pencil will no longer make the mark."*3A*

1. I can't understand you, Tami replied into the receiver of the phone.

2. I won't be able to help you, Cindy explained. I have to catch my bus.

3. Miguel's mother said, You shouldn't always answer with just one word like nope or huh.

4. Let me cite an example from Tobin's article:

   The issue cannot be settled by the decision on the new law. Although the decision will clear up some outstanding legal questions, it will not be a complete resolution because too many people still misunderstand the reasons why it is necessary.

   In addition, we will not be able to settle the funding issues before the deadline for a smooth project start. For this reason the project will be behind schedule before it begins.

5. During the argument Rick countered, Your solution is not acceptable to anyone except you.

6. As Tracy left the stage you could hear her mutter the lines, Don't yell at me; don't even talk to me.

7. Akeo's answer in the interview included his mother's exact words, She said, You will always be a winner. Now that I really feel like one, I believe her.

8. Don't eat any more cookie dough, Ellie insisted to her brother. We need all of it to finish the cookies.

9. The President stated that he would propose a new economic policy which would help deal with the financial concerns of many businesses.

10. We can't fill all of the positions until next week, Miss Jarvis explained.

The answers are in the back of the text-workbook.

EXERCISE 3B
Chapter 5   *QUOTATION MARKS*

RULES 1–3

- Insert quotation marks in the following examples and write the rule number and letter from the Compact Quotation Mark Summary above each quotation mark you insert.
- The uses involve Rules 1, 2, and 3.
- In the last five sentences one does not need quotation marks.

Example: We will begin the lesson at the beginning of Chapter 3, *1A*"Explorers in the New World.*1A*"

1. Will you please set the table? asked Mrs. Martinez as she prepared the holiday meal.

2. I cannot believe, Gary insisted, that you have changed so little since I saw you last.

3. Please make sure that your memo does not make any mistakes with to, two, and too.

4. You will find your answer in the next to the last chapter, Patterns for Change.

5. The band played When We Part as the last song at the dance.

6. The commission chairperson directed the members, Let's begin the session today with a look at Chapter 4, Recommended Alternatives.

7. We cannot afford to ignore the recommendations, the chairperson stated. The plan must be carried out right away and funding must be provided on a continuing basis.

8. The judge's remarks on the suit were included in the article.

   Nowhere in the testimony did I find just cause for the actions which the defendant took. On the other hand, I cannot say that his actions were not provoked by the circumstances surrounding the case. The statute is not clear on this specific point in question.

   My examination of the case law yields no clear direction. For these reasons, the suit will be dropped; however, further action on other grounds will be possible.

9. The producers were not successful trying to find a buyer for the new series, Who's At Home?

10. The most useful information was in *Time*, A Portrait of a Leader.

11. McClaren offered a solution to the problem with the rotating helix inference pattern, but it was too theoretical to be useful.

12. I can't wait, Theresa muttered as she scooted out of line. I have to check in at the boarding gate, or I'll miss my plane.

13. Pete wrote the lyrics to She's Got the Feelin' one month before Midori completed the music.

14. When she left the party, Nancy did not show her concern, but later she voiced it to everyone with her sarcastic remarks.

15. The latest issue of *Newslook* has a review of the article, Foreign Policy: Points to Ponder.

The answers are in the back of the text-workbook.

HYPHEN

Chapter 6 The Word Connector

For many writers the hyphen is an elusive punctuation mark. Some general rules apply, but they have several exceptions. In addition, writers use the hyphen routinely to make new combinations of words. The hyphen and apostrophe are punctuation marks working with words while many of the other marks deal with the language at a sentence level. Some hyphen uses are formal and consistent; others depend on situations or meanings.

Words with hyphens will also change. For some uses the separate words are written together with a hyphen for a period of time, and then later as the combination becomes familiar to most readers, the words are combined into a single word. For example, at some point in history the word *motor* became associated with *cycle* to name the combination of the internal combustion engine with a bicycle. It was first written as *motor cycle*. Later it developed a special sense and became *motor-cycle*. After some time it was combined to the present form of *motorcycle*. We also use the hyphen on a temporary basis to form modifiers that explain our terms. For instance, terms like *high-pressure job* or *no-fault insurance* are coined in specific instances to show relationships for readers.

The hyphen preserves word connections when a word appears on two lines because space is not available. The hyphen is also a mechanical device to clarify what would be confusing if written otherwise. Use the hyphen as a connector to help your reader avoid confusion with specific words.

COMBINED WORD FORMS
Chapter 6   *HYPHEN*

LEARNING OBJECTIVES

After your study of Hyphen Rule 1, you will be able to:
• Insert hyphens correctly in combined word forms.
• Label hyphen uses to indicate which type of word form is used.

RULE 1: Use hyphens in COMBINED word forms.

A. Compound nouns

B. Compound adjectives

C. Combined phrases

A. make-believe
   money-maker
   close-up

B. high-pressure hose
   government-owned equipment
   short-term loan
   10-yard gain

C. hole-in-the-wall gang
   stick-in-the-mud
   never-say-die
   mother-in-law

Fold out the Compact Hyphen Summary in the back of the text-workbook so you can see it while you read the explanations and work on the exercises.

HYPHEN—COMBINING

A. Compound nouns

You have probably written some combination of words and wondered if you needed a hyphen. One of the features of English is its flexibility allowing for new combinations of existing words that make additional new words unnecessary. For example, because we can combine words like *by* and *product* into *by-product*, we do not have to invent a new word. Certain word combinations are invented as new ideas or inventions become available. Writers must invent or "coin" new words as they attempt to express their ideas.

The usual sequence of these events is to take two or more separate words and hyphenate them, thereby connecting them. As the combination becomes familiar over time, writers drop the hyphen, and the words are written as one word. Sometimes this transition is rapid, and in only a few years the new spelling is established. Other times the transition takes many years, and occasionally some combinations never make the switch.

Words may be combined with a hyphen to help the reader understand the intended meaning for a particular instance, but the word combination is only temporary or not widely used. We make these temporary and potentially permanent combinations work as nouns, modifiers, and combined phrases. For example, we use the words *go* and *between* when we are discussing negotiations or mediation. When we need a word to describe a person who will represent one party's interest to another or help settle disagreements, we use the term *go-between*. This becomes a very descriptive word combination for the person we are discussing. When we use the terms as a phrase to describe an action, we do not hyphenate the combination. Notice how in the first sentence *go between* describes an action. In the second sentence *go-between* is a word combination used to name the role Tom will play. These noun combinations are hyphenated.

Verb	As she follows the trail she will *go between* the stand of oak trees and the creek.
Noun	Tom will act as a *go-between* when we finally get the former partners to the meeting.

Noun combinations may include more than two words. These combinations such as *mother-in-law* are discussed under combined phrases in Rule 1C.

B. Compound adjectives

Compound adjectives offer one of the greatest opportunities for a writer to invent words. Remember that an adjective is a word which describes a noun. The hyphen can make a difference in meaning.

a little used car

a little-used car

The hyphen lets the reader know that the car was not used very much. The phrase written without the hyphen tells the reader that the used car is small. These modifying combinations occur frequently in our writing.

These modifying phrases may consist of general word types in several combinations. Here is a sampling of the types and the ways that they can be combined.

cross-country trip	(*cross* plus word)
half-baked idea	(*half* plus word)
blue-green paint	(color combination)
high-pressure pump	(*high, low* plus describer)
still-capable leader	(adverb plus word)
well-known personality	(*well, ill, little, lesser,...* plus past participle)
quasi-professional activity	(*quasi* plus describer)
decision-making process	(noun plus present participle)
fifty-odd spectators	(number plus *odd*)
ten-mile radius	(number plus unit of measure)
all-around champion	(*all* plus word)
able-bodied worker	(*able, coarse, straight, even ...* plus past participle)
25-foot ladder	(number plus noun)

This list is not comprehensive; many similar words also work. They use hyphens in combination with various word forms to show the modification. Hyphenate the compound adjectives consistently and clearly.

C. Combined phrases

Sometimes certain words in phrases become so linked that they act as a unit. The phrase becomes a noun or an adjective and is used as if it were one word. For instance, the words *stay, at,* and *home,* can be combined to become a modifier.

She spent her weekends working around the house; she had developed a real stay-at-home habit.

The hyphen will also help you make a one-word unit out of several words.

state-of-the-art equipment
up-to-date information
devil-may-care attitude
never-to-be-forgotten incident
off-the-record remark
life-and-death concern
pay-as-you-go approach
hit-and-miss manner

SUMMARY

Rule 1 for hyphen use is challenging because of the many possible variations for word combinations. You can combine words to make nouns or form modifiers. Some phrases become so common that they become almost like a single word to most readers. The hyphen allows familiar words and phrases to combine and serve in new roles with new meanings.

EXERCISE 1

Chapter 6 *HYPHEN*

RULE 1

- Insert hyphens in the following sentences and write the rule number and letter from the Compact Hyphen Summary above each hyphen you insert.
- All the uses involve Rule 1.
- In the last five sentences one does not need a hyphen.

Example: We will not give the *1A* go-ahead for the project until the financing is arranged.

1. You will not be able to buy state of the art gifts at the department store.

2. With the coming of spring we will not be able to use the motor driven raking machine from last year.

3. The double check of all the instruments will happen on the night shift.

4. She always approaches projects with a devil may care attitude.

5. The typical low volume, well designed cap monitor will not be available until the beginning of fall.

6. Even though he is a high ranking sprinter, his efforts in the 10 kilometer race will depend on his long distance conditioning.

7. We will be making long term commitments to the new teams as soon as their rankings are established.

8. They teased him about being an "over the hill grump."

9. The photographer switched lenses on the camera and adjusted the lighting to prepare for the close ups of the family.

10. The engineers designed the mechanism to be a self actuating, solid lever device that can be used in a variety of situations.

11. At the end of each chapter you will find a cross referenced list of the most important ideas.

12. Nothing can match the thirst quenching ability of water fresh from a spring.

13. Be sure that your manuscript has a one inch margin on all edges.

14. Even with all of the possibilities, the leaders could not agree on a new rental policy for the group.

15. Sylvia won the award as the best all around athlete at the track meet.

The answers are in the back of the text-workbook.

INTERNAL WORD FORMS
Chapter 6   *HYPHEN*

LEARNING OBJECTIVES

After your study of Hyphen Rule 2, you will be able to:
• Insert hyphens correctly in internal word forms.
• Label hyphen uses to indicate which type of internal form is used—prefixes or word separations.

RULE 2: Use hyphens in INTERNAL word forms.

A. Some prefixes

A. (misreading)   re-create
   (capital letter)   anti-British
   (ex- and self-)   ex-president
   (double vowel)   semi-independent

B. Word separations
   (end of a line)

B. The legislature will not appropriate the funds.

(Note: Consult a current dictionary when using hyphens with prefixes or for word divisions.)

Fold out the Compact Hyphen Summary in the back of the text-workbook so you can see it while you read the explanations and work on the exercises.

A. Some
prefixes

Generally prefixes are not separated by hyphens, but some circumstances make hyphens necessary for clarity. With these exceptions insert a hyphen between a prefix and a root word. These exceptions usually prevent the reader's confusion.

The examples on the Compact Hyphen Summary show some of these exceptions. We hyphenate the prefix *re-* when we attach it to *create* because without the hyphen the word has another meaning.

re-create to create again

recreate to participate in an activity

If you add a prefix to a word beginning with a capital letter, use the hyphen to keep the capitalization from coming in the middle of the word by including a hyphen.

un-American	**NOT**	unAmerican
anti-British		antiBritish

When *self* is a prefix, use a hyphen. When *self* is the root word as in *selfless,* do not use a hyphen. Some authorities suggest that you avoid the uses of *ex-* and use *former* as a separate word instead.

ex-president (former president)

self-governing board

Sometimes the letter ending a prefix is the same as the letter beginning the root word. This often happens with vowels. Unfortunately, the hyphen rules in these instances are not consistent. Some double vowel combinations seem acceptable while others do not. For example, *reeducate* is considered a correct form while *ultraactive* is not. A recent dictionary will be your best guide; however, this chart may help.

If the prefix ends with:

i and a use a hyphen
e and o do not use a hyphen

Note these examples:
semi-independent
ultra-active
reemphasize
cooperate

There are exceptions to these rules. One dictionary lists *de-emphasize* and *co-op.* These principles work in general, but you should check your current dictionary.

B. Word
separations

Even with word processors and "intelligent" typewriters, you will often need to divide a word at the end of a line and then continue it on the next line. The hyphen shows that the parts are still connected as one word. This division should always be made between syllables.

> We will not be available for the funding confer-
> ence on Thursday.

Although this is a simple rule, keep enough of the word on each line for the reader to grasp the meaning easily. Usually single letters are not left alone on either line. Some style guides also recommend carrying at least three letters to the next line.

> The pilot project will be necessary to meet certifi-
> cation requirements.

Many style guides include additional guidelines for word division. Always use a hyphen to show the word division.

SUMMARY

Hyphens are used with some prefixes to separate the prefix from the root word and make the word's meaning clear. The other need for an internal hyphen occurs when a word cannot be completed on one line and must be continued on another line.

EXERCISE 2A
Chapter 6   *HYPHEN*

RULE 2

> ● Insert hyphens in the following sentences and write the rule number and letter from the Compact Hyphen Summary above each hyphen you insert.
> ● All the uses involve Rule 2.

Example: Everyone wished that he would change his semi ⁻indirect methods and be more
            accurate.

1. The new board will be composed of semi independent contractors.

2. It will be necessary to re create the tax records that were lost in the fire.

3. As you review the report, we hope that you will find that the mater
      ials are sufficient.

4. The ambassador's remarks carried a clearly anti American tone.

5. In the oldest notebook you will see that she patiently and dili
      gently kept records of the trip to the West.

6. The self made millionaire will be leading the conference.

7. Our ex mayor will not be attending the dedication ceremony this year.

8. The mid January date will allow plenty of time for addi
      tional planning.

9. The anti intellectual mood gradually changed as more people understood the issues
      involved.

10. The clerk re marked the ticket in time for the sale to begin.

The answers are in the back of the text-workbook.

EXERCISE 2B   RULES 1–2
Chapter 6   *HYPHEN*

- Insert hyphens in the following sentences and write the rule number and letter from the Compact Hyphen Summary above each hyphen you insert.
- The uses involve Rules 1 and 2.
- In the last five sentences one does not need a hyphen.

Example: We can no longer consider your make^{1B}-believe explanations useful or even entertaining.

1. Does your brother in law plan to sell his boat and trailer?

2. No one can predict whether the matter of fact approach she used will please the customer.

3. Do you think the jury will be able to ignore the indisput able facts the lawyer outlined in the speech?

4. We will be developing several low cost options for the project.

5. The historians will have to re create all of the documents from the fragments that survived the fire.

6. I believe that Jose is ready with an up to date report.

7. If you will include a self addressed envelope with your request, you are more likely to get a quick response.

8. When the vice consul of the embassy approved the plans, she considered some of them short term solutions, and she considered others long term relief.

9. The professor was an expert in post Civil War history.

10. The engineer described the invention as an air cooled, high capacity power unit.

11. The high priced, old fashioned materials will not work for the new design.

12. In the case of the older items on the shelf, the clerks will have to wait until mid January to reorganize the stock.

13. The trans Alaska pipeline is able to provide a steady supply of crude oil for U.S. motorists.

14. We must not create a recreation site that will harm the endangered species.

15. After he was elected secretary treasurer of the club, Kuang-Fu realized that he would have most of the work.

The answers are in the back of the text-workbook.

MECHANICS
Chapter 6   *HYPHEN*

LEARNING OBJECTIVES

After your study of Hyphen Rule 3, you will be able to:
- Insert hyphens correctly in mechanical situations.
- Label hyphen uses to indicate which mechanical situation is used.

RULE 3: Use hyphens for MECHANICS.

A. Numbers

A. twenty-three
two-fifths
A 4-2 victory really pleased the coach.
pages 234-238

B. Unusual or extended pronunciation

B. G-g-glad you could make it.
Say a-a-a-h.

C. Letters as letters

C. The spelling champ spelled *receive*
r-e-c-e-i-v-e to win the round.

D. Suspended forms

D. She taught a group of six- and seven-
year-olds.
Lumber may be purchased in 8-, 12-, and
16-foot lengths.

Fold out the Compact Hyphen Summary in the back of the text-workbook so you can see it while you read the explanations and work on the exercises.

HYPHEN—MECHANICS

A. Numbers

Some numbers need hyphens when expressed in words. When you spell the words for the numbers 21 through 99, you should hyphenate those word combinations.

> thirty-two
> eighty-four
> fifty-six
> seventy-nine

Word combinations for fractions also require hyphens to separate the numerators and the denominators.

> three-fifths
> two-sevenths
> nine-thirteenths
> seven-eighths

However, if either the numerator or the denominator of the fraction already contains a hyphen, do not use a hyphen between the numerator and the denominator.

> twenty-three hundredths   23/100
>
> nine thirty-seconds   9/32

RANGES AND RATIOS. At times you may need to write about a range of numbers. For example, you may need to express a range of years such as 1990-1992 or 1860-1864. You may need to show a range of pages such as pages 247-254.

Another number usage of the hyphen is to show a ratio. Generally a ratio is indicated by a colon, but frequently a hyphen is used to show a score of a ball game or event.

> The Breezers won the 55-44 game even though some key players were out with injuries.

> The 3-2 victory was a crucial win for the Pacers.

B. Unusual pronunciation

The accepted way of writing word hesitations, stuttering, and extended vowel sounds in text is to use hyphens. It is one mechanical tool used to duplicate a pattern of speech in writing. This form is used regularly in fiction writing.

> You'll be the t-t-top speller in the class if you win the contest.

> I-I-I'm so confused.

> Open your mouth and say a-a-ah.

C. Letters as letters

The hyphen may show letters as letters rather than as a letter combination forming a word. When you need to write the spelling of a word to indicate that it is being spelled, you can use the hyp separate and call attention to each of the letters.

> Remember that you must note the difference between *t-o-o* and *t-w-o* when you write.

> Italic type may also be used when available to show the use o ters as letters.

D. Suspended forms

Using a hyphen to show a suspended form can be handy. Someti two prefixes or combined words are applied to the same base wo

> The new bank will make long- and short-term loans.

In this case the combined adjectives *long* and *short* combine wi *term* to modify *loans*.

> At the nursery the trees were sold in 1-, 5-, and 10-gallon buckets.

> We will not need both 13- and 14- year-old students to serve on the advisory council.

SUMMARY

Hyphens are used to show connections within words to the reader. The thorough writer will use them consistently to write out numbers, to show unusual pronunciation or hesitation in speech, to show letters referred to as letters, and to show suspended words and parts of words.

Hyphen uses are not often noticed unless they are missing. Without hyphens readers can be slowed, distracted, or even confused. In some cases the hyphen can change the meaning of words or phrases. Remember a current dictionary will reflect the current trends and show the changes in how words are written.

EXERCISE 3A
Chapter 6 *HYPHEN*

RULE 3

● Insert hyphens in the following sentences and write the rule number and letter from the Compact Hyphen Summary above each hyphen you insert.
● All the uses involve Rule 3.

Example: The major problem for the new committee was raising the funds to pay for the
          twenty-four outstanding bills.

           3A

1. You will find that working with twenty five children in a preschool class is a tremendous challenge.

2. The two thirds majority needed to pass the bill will not be available until Thursday.

3. When you paint the sign, be sure to spell the word *Eddie's* E d d i e 's and not E d d y 's.

4. Sheila was so shaken by the accident that her conversation was unusual, "I I I couldn't stop in t t time."

5. You will have to carry both 25 and 50 pound bags as you load the truck.

6. The Panthers picked up a 4 3 win on their way to the championship.

7. Even though you do not pronounce all the letters *k n o t* is definitely a different word than *n a u g h t*.

8. My graphic presentation will reflect about two fifths of the complete written version of the report.

9. Helen replied, "I w w w will not accept your apology."

10. At the end of the survey the first, second, and third ranked factors will need further study.

The answers are in the back of the text-workbook.

EXERCISE 3B
Chapter 6   *HYPHEN*

RULES 1–3

- Insert hyphens in the following sentences and write the rule number and letter from the Compact Hyphen Summary above each hyphen you insert.
- The uses involve all three rules.
- In the last five sentences one does not need a hyphen.

Example: You will have to find a well¹ᴮ-proven technique, or your efforts will be pointless.

1. The club kept one third of its money in an interest bearing checking account and the other two thirds in a short term certificate of deposit.

2. The fans continued to cheer as the teams went into overtime to settle the 2 2 score.

3. He slowed the car as he approached the 35 mile an hour speed zone.

4. The self proclaimed leader of the group provided a clear focus for their efforts.

5. Even though it was once stained, you will have to re treat the lumber before it can be used on the new deck.

6. The test was completed at 10, 30, and 60 minute intervals.

7. The need for a pro African policy was made clear to all of the delegates.

8. Carlson had no idea that *wrought iron* was spelled w r o u g h t.

9. Jill's brother in law met her at the mall to help her shop for her husband's gift.

10. With his grandfather's help, John was able to develop a pay as you go plan to pay for his new car.

11. Frank was elected secretary treasurer of the group because he owned a computer to help handle the lengthy correspond ence and finances.

12. Without a minimum water level following the drought, the reservoir owned by the city could not meet the water needs of the small community.

13. The well known actor rejected the part because he would be in fewer than one fifth of the major scenes.

14. U u ugh! I can't stand the taste of that toothpaste.

15. As Betsy studied the weather beaten old building for her photographic session, she saw several artistic possibil ities for the magazine cover.

The answers are in the back of the text-workbook.

PARENTHESES

Chapter 7 The Major Detour

Parentheses can be a flexible tool in the writer's punctuation tool kit. They signal the reader that the information they enclose is extra or optional. Since parentheses interrupt a sentence, a wise author considers their use carefully.

Remember that the parentheses are the strongest interruption in the stairsteps of punctuation. They disrupt the reader the most. Often they provide a simple yet effective way to express supplemental information in your writing. They can set off references to other parts of the writing such as illustrations. They can be used to interrupt briefly for a definition, and they can enclose comments about main information. Use parentheses to add information to your writing and direct your reader.

INTERRUPTIONS
Chapter 7   *PARENTHESES*

LEARNING OBJECTIVES

After your study of Parentheses Rule 1, you will be able to:
• Insert parentheses correctly in interrupting situations.
• Label parentheses uses to show the type of interruption used.

RULE 1: Use parentheses to set off INTERRUPTIONS.

A. Explanations
   (words, phrases, or clauses)

A. As you study the report, note the results (including statistics).
   As you study the report (including all supporting material and statistics), note the results.
   As you study the report, note the results. (Be sure to study the tables.)

B. Comments

B. You will find him working (oddly enough) in the garage.

C. Examples

C. Several of the senior players (Ellen, Jackie, Susan) will continue until the end of the season.

D. Abbreviations

D. The CRT (cathode ray tube) has had an important impact on several technological changes.

E. Transitional expressions
   (i.e., e.g., that is, for example)

E. Several artifacts (e.g., a pot, a hammer, a digging tool) were found at the new site.
   The altered committee (i.e., the new officers and members) will develop the new plan.

Fold out the Compact Parentheses Summary in the back of the text-workbook so you can see it while you read the explanations and work on the exercises.

PARENTHESES—INTERRUPTIONS

A. **Explanatory material**

You may interrupt your regular sentence patterns with a pair of parentheses. Rule 1 refers to including additional material connected to the main sentence. Sometimes in these situations the material you enclose in the parentheses will be more specific than the general terms you used in the main sentence.

> In the index you will find more references (over twenty) to President Nixon than to other presidents.

Using the phrase *over twenty* in addition to the word *more* helps the reader understand the size of the difference. Do not try to cover up sloppy writing by using parentheses. Try to add information to the general term with specific clarification. The information inside the parentheses can be phrases or even complete sentences.

> In the future please forward your correspondence to the Adjustments Department (formerly the Customer Credit Office), and we will be glad to respond accordingly.

> Although you will find ample storage in the warehouse (it is closer to your facility), you will have to provide for your own security.

B. **Comments**

Parentheses are a great tool for the writer who likes to comment. You can include your comments on the text within parentheses. Be careful, however. Overusing parentheses can become distracting. On the other hand, your comments within your text can personalize the text and add variety.

> After you work on your project this weekend (as I am sure you will), be certain to close your computer account.

> William was worried about his father's health (which he certainly had every right to be) even though the rest of the family ignored the problem.

C. **Examples**

Sometimes you may want to include some examples of a general term to make sure your reader understands your meaning. One way is to include some of these examples within a pair of parentheses. Remember that parentheses separate the interrupting material from the sentence the most abruptly.

> Be sure to study all of the rules (off sides, out of bounds, time limits) that are in your guidebook.

Do not use parentheses this way as a substitute for clarity. If you find your sentence is not clear without the information within the parentheses, rewrite the sentence to include it. Remember that putting parentheses around examples or other information makes the information optional.

> If you can complete the uniform orders (hats, jerseys, and pants) by next Friday, we will be able to make arrangements for the shipping.

D. Abbreviations

Parentheses also clarify abbreviations and acronyms frequently used in business and technical writing. Many are familiar ones such as CRT, FAA, CIA, and CPU. The writer must make sure readers understand them. Technically they are only acronyms if they are pronounced as a word; otherwise, they are abbreviations. (For example, we spell out C-R-T rather than say "curt," yet we pronounce a police Special Weapons and Tactics team as a SWAT team, making this an acronym.)

Some of these acronyms eventually become so familiar that they become words. *Scuba* and *radar* are examples. (By the way their definitions are *S*elf-*C*ontained *U*nderwater *B*reathing *A*pparatus and *RA*dio *D*etecting *A*nd *R*anging.) When this happens people often forget the original term. For some technicians or people in government and industry some terms also become part of the specialized vocabulary, which those people working in the field understand readily.

Although some writing guides say you should avoid these shortened versions, they are appropriate for specific readers of a particular piece of writing. A manual written for skilled technicians, for instance, will have readers familiar with the abbreviations for particular equipment. These specialized readers will have little difficulty, but you still must use parentheses to help your reader.

> In your estimate please note the LCC (life cycle cost).

> The ECU (electronic control unit) will be tested before installation.

The abbreviation may be included in the parentheses, or the explanation or definition may be included within the parentheses. Both ways are frequently used.

> The new CPU (central processing unit) is 50 percent more powerful than the older model.

> The new central processing unit (CPU) is 50 percent more powerful than the older model.

Remain consistent within a document. Using the first method helps the reader because the reader does not have to reverse the order after this first reference.

E. Transitional expressions

Parentheses are sometimes used with the special transitional expressions. The Latin abbreviations *e.g.* and *i.e.* are always followed by a comma; however, the punctuation mark before them can be a comma, a colon, a semicolon, a dash, or parentheses. (See the other chapters for the use of these marks.) Note the table below, which appears in the other the chapters too. It has the abbreviations, their meanings, and English meanings.

Latin term	Abbreviation	English equivalent
exempli gratia	e.g.	for example
id est	i.e.	that is or namely

The writer must make a choice based on how strongly to separate the material from the rest of the sentence. Mild separations get commas, semicolons, and colons. Strong separations get dashes. The most abrupt use parentheses.

> We will have to make the plans more specific (i.e., provide a schedule, a method of organizing volunteers, and a budget.)

These separations can be used with their English counterparts as well.

> You cannot make all the decisions right away (for example, the color scheme must wait until the lighting design is complete.)

SUMMARY

Parentheses can separate interruptions from the rest of the sentence. These interruptions may be explanations, comments, examples, abbreviations, or material introduced with transitional expressions. The information placed within the parentheses must not be essential to the meaning or clarity of the sentence.

EXERCISE 1
Chapter 7 *PARENTHESES*

RULE 1

- Insert parentheses in the following examples and write the rule number and letter from the Compact Parentheses Summary above each parenthesis you insert.
- All the uses involve Rule 1.

Example: Your income was reported to the IRS *1D*(Internal Revenue Service*1D*).

1. When you file the PRS Proposed Reservation System form make sure that all the information in Part IV is complete.

2. The administration department has become a catch-all for many organizations e.g., accounting, security, printing, and others.

3. No further action can be taken on the DLR direct labor report because the increase in budget is not available until after the first of the year.

4. Her words began to annoy the audience including many of her former friends and allies as she made her way from point to point.

5. How can we develop an interface with the new equipment i.e., how can what we have work with the additional machines we plan to buy?

6. The team's equipment including even extra jerseys and practice uniforms remains the property of the league.

7. As the students began the art course, they found they needed supplies brushes, pencils, erasers, and paints to begin the first project.

8. When you complete your monthly labor report, include all the data from your organization. Be certain to include the remaining budget, hours worked, and units shipped.

9. The committee members Margaret, Gale, Gary, and Al will attend the meeting if you feel their help is needed.

10. I cannot see any way to break the pattern of failure unless we restructure the department I know you don't want that.

The answers are in the back of the text-workbook.

MECHANICAL POINTING
Chapter 7 *PARENTHESES*

LEARNING OBJECTIVES

After your study of Parentheses Rule 2, you will be able to:
* Insert parentheses correctly to indicate the mechanical pointings.
* Label parentheses uses to indicate the pointing is a reference or citation.

RULE 2: Use parentheses for MECHANICAL POINTING.

A. References

A. The performance is outstanding (see Figure 1).
Profits were higher this quarter. (See Table 7.)

B. Citations

B. As you can conclude from her study (Smith, 1987), the research seems complete.

Fold out the Compact Parentheses Summary in the back of the text-workbook so you can see it while you read the explanations and work on the exercises.

PARENTHESES—POINTING

As you help guide your readers, you may need to point to parts of an article, report, or book or direct them to another section or paragraph. You may want to refer the reader to an appendix, a figure, or a table that adds information. You will also have a need to cite references to works that other authors have written. Parentheses provide one method for you to guide your reader.

A. References

You may need to direct your reader to another element in your writing such as a table, a photo, a figure, or an illustration. It could also be a reference to another chapter or section. Writing of all types is filled with these mechanisms of reference.

Direct your reader by placing the reference between a pair of parentheses. You may include the words *see* or *refer to* along with the reference, or you may simply place the reference between the parentheses.

> The final vibration test confirmed the previous results. (See Table 7.)

> Other factors (refer to Figure 7) influenced the outcome of the election.

> Annual sales summaries (Tables 4–11 in Appendix B) provide the needed information for the report.

B. Citations

You have many methods of citing another work available to you. There are footnotes, endnotes, and several variations of each. One of the easiest methods of referencing documentation is where the author's last name and the year of publication are included in parentheses after the idea or quotation to which it refers. The author's works are listed in the bibliography alphabetically by author and then by year to complete the reference.

> According to Sandoval (Sandoval, 1990) we cannot accept all of the alternatives. Some are too dangerous.

Follow a specific style if you have a requirement from a particular editor or instructor. You will probably see this method of citation in your academic reading.

EXERCISE 2A   RULE 2
Chapter 7   *PARENTHESES*

- Insert parentheses in the following examples and write the rule number and letter from the Compact Parentheses Summary above each parenthesis you insert.
- All the uses involve Rule 2.

Example: The membership rule *2A*(Section 2 paragraph 7 *2A*) clearly states the eligibility for all players.

1. The minimum value is 27.5 pounds; it has been established by solid experiments Wilson, 1987.

2. The most reliable information points toward the conclusion that the rates will decline next year. See Figure 7.

3. The main points were made in the conclusion, but other useful information was in the special matrix and the references see Section 4.

4. You will find the results detailed in the accompanying tables see Appendix 1.

5. The data in the study revealed a lower worker absence rate Janforth, 1990.

6. As you complete the installation of the motor cover paragraphs 7 through 12, keep all other parts out of the way to avoid confusion.

7. Your use of the initial meter settings Table 3 will help make the test a valid one.

8. The relationships of the various chemicals were established by earlier experiments Amstad, 1966 while the complete matrix was described later by Laura Smith Smith, 1977.

9. In the early stages of your work Chapters 1-20 you will need more time; in the later stages Chapters 21-38 you will not.

10. The reliability of the new process has been confirmed Hancock, 1988, but it is still not widely used.

The answers are in the back of the text-workbook.

EXERCISE 2B
Chapter 7   *PARENTHESES*

RULES 1–2

- Insert parentheses in the following examples and write the rule number and letter from the Compact Parentheses Summary above each parenthesis you insert.
- All the uses involve Rules 1 and 2.
- In the last five sentences one does not need parentheses.

Example: With the correct information we can now calculate the ROI ^{1D}(return on investment^{1D}) for the new equipment.

1. The newest experiments Westfall, 1990 confirm the results of the studies done by Betty Campbell Campbell, 1987.

2. William Hewlitt was recently elected president of ICBA International Congress of Business Associates.

3. With few exceptions the pattern repeats regardless of temperature changes. See Figure 6.

4. The IDU International Detailers Union provides scholarships for several college students.

5. While the negotiations continue, you will have to keep most points confidential i.e., you cannot issue press releases and you cannot make stock trades.

6. The champions of the NFC National Football Conference and AFC American Football Conference meet every year in the Superbowl in January.

7. The new model will include several new features, but the most notable is a TAB total access bracket.

8. The students on the committee have completed the project I never doubted that they would in record time.

9. Many newer cars have an ABS antilock braking system as standard equipment; others have it as an option.

10. Additional research following Answeil's discovery Patten, 1987 confirmed the results and lead to a more useful product.

11. Hundreds of antiques furniture, tools, lanterns, pictures, and kitchen utensils were auctioned when the old barn was torn down.

12. The job application process and hiring procedure at most companies are governed by regulations from the EEOC Equal Employment Opportunity Commission.

13. As you wax the car, be sure to polish the wheel lug nuts too.

14. If you believe Okano's idea Okano, 1988, then you will also have to agree with Winston's refinements Winston, 1990.

15. You will find the corresponding data in detail later in the chapter. See Table II.

The answers are in the back of the text-workbook.

NUMBERS
Chapter 7   *PARENTHESES*

LEARNING OBJECTIVES

After your study of Parentheses Rule 3, you will be able to:
- Insert parentheses correctly when they are associated with numbers.
- Label parentheses uses to indicate which use with numbers is appropriate.

RULE 3: Use parentheses to list or repeat NUMBERS.

A. List within a sentence
   (letters as an alternate)

A. The class president made plans for all the spring activities: (1) the carnival, (2) the final dance, and (3) the special talent show.

   The class president made plans for all the spring activities: (a) the carnival, (b) the final dance, and (c) the special talent show.

B. Repetition for accuracy

B. Please provide sixty (60) dozen of the new washers.

Fold out the Compact Parentheses Summary in the back of the text-workbook so you can see it while you read the explanations and work on the exercises.

PARENTHESES—NUMBERS

A. Lists in sentences

Parentheses enclose numbers or letters when they are used in lists within sentences.

> For the meeting we will have to complete all of the following: (1) prepare the budget, (2) develop a strategy, and (3) implement the specific plan.

> We will need to provide for the following problems: (a) adequate funding, (b) safety regulations, and (c) proper notification.

B. Repetition for accuracy

Sometimes in legal or scientific work one number must not be mistaken for another. When this is required, the number is usually spelled out in words and then repeated in figures enclosed in parentheses.

> The formula requires exactly three (3) milliliters of benzene.

> Please complete the order for twenty-seven (27) sets of the instruction manuals.

> Remember that repeating the number in parentheses is only necessary when accuracy is essential.

EXERCISE 3A
Chapter 7   *PARENTHESES*

RULE 3

- Insert parentheses in the following examples and write the rule number and letter from the Compact Parentheses Summary above each parenthesis you insert.
- All the uses involve Rule 3.
- In the last five sentences one does not need parentheses.

Example: Please complete the order for eighteen $\overset{3B}{(}18\overset{3B}{)}$ 4-door sedans for the service fleet.

1. The team will need several new tactics for the new season: 1 it will have to develop a stronger defense, 2 it will have to develop better scouting reports, and 3 it will need a motivational leader.

2. The lease reads, "The Lessee/User shall pay to Acme, Inc. the base rent of twelve thousand dollars $12,000 in three 3 installments."

3. We have prevented further damage by taking the following preventive actions: 1 buying reinforced window frames, 2 installing new latches, and 3 replacing older hinges.

4. We need to go further because we cannot find the following information: 1 last year's figures, 2 enough information on our competitors and 3 the research on the new product.

5. The official report read, "The crash occurred on lap thirty-three 33 of the race."

6. As the figures were compiled, the winners were decided because they had more than seventeen correct responses.

7. The folklore about the mansion said that it was 1 haunted by the first owner, 2 sold every two years because of water problems, and 3 almost destroyed because it was not properly constructed.

8. Most nutritionists still agree that balance in your diet is achieved by a a variety of foods, b moderation in that not all foods are from the same groups, and c skillful selection and cooking.

9. Please clarify your order. Do you want four 4 dozen or forty 40 dozen of the Model 41B?

10. You will be able to pass the certification exam by 1 studying all of the material, 2 committing the study guide to memory, and 3 getting a good night's sleep the night before.

The answers are in the back of the text-workbook.

EXERCISE 3B

Chapter 7   *PARENTHESES*

RULES 1–3

- Insert parentheses in the following examples and write the rule number and letter from the Compact Parentheses Summary above each parenthesis you insert.
- The uses involve all three parentheses rules.
- In the last five sentences one does not need parentheses.

Example: Will you be needing all of the tools *1C* (hammers, screwdrivers, saws, planes, and pliers *1C*) for the project?

1. The juniors on the team Susan, Katrina, Natalie, and Patty will be returning for another season next year.

2. Miss Sanchez' order called for two hundred 200 of the 16-valve units.

3. Spectators will be allowed to use the reserved seating later in the game. After all the hassle no one will want to sit there anyway.

4. The sale of the company was approved by the SEC Securities Exchange Commission because all of the requirements were met at the time of the sale.

5. As the planning commission considers the application, several factors must be studied: 1 the effect of changes on jobs, 2 the need for additional water facilities, and 3 the time frame for completing the project.

6. Carol Simpson will lead the new committee I hope she does not meet opposition and complete the development effort.

7. The study which lead to the recommendation Barnes, 1988 clarified all of the issues.

8. The compiled data see p. 52 clearly establishes the need for an additional hospital in the area.

9. The engineers calculated the LCC Life Cycle Cost for the fleet of new airplanes.

10. Using extreme caution and patience i.e., not starting too early will allow you to solve many of the problems without additional testing.

11. No additional funds will be available from the Historical Foundation Fund for the rebuilding of the old building.

12. In addition to the preliminary results see Chapter 3, the complete data taken during the test show a clear improvement in the water quality. See Appendix B.

13. All of the equipment for the team including all playing gear and uniforms was delayed at the airport causing a rush to prepare for the game.

14. The FCC Federal Communications Commission will need to approve the new licenses for the transmitter, but the operation will still be on schedule.

15. Preparations for the project will include the following: 1 funding, 2 approvals, and 3 detailed site plans.

The answers are in the back of the text-workbook.

END MARKS

Chapter 8   Finally

This chapter covers marking the end of sentences and using end marks in other situations. In most situations the end marks close the units of thought.

LEARNING OBJECTIVES

After your study of End Marks Rule 1, you will be able to:
- Insert periods correctly at the end of sentences and other mechanical uses.
- Label period uses to show that period use is appropriate.

RULE 1: Use PERIODS to mark the end of a sentence or unit of thought.

A. Statements	A. He graduated in 1989.
B. Commands	B. Close the door.
C. Itemized lists	C.
• Numbered items	• These will be the key items you need:
	1. canteen
	2. flashlight
	3. sleeping bag
• Lettered items	• We will need the following:
	a. garden tools
	b. seeds
	c. willingness to work
D. Decimals	D. The new budget is 9.4 percent higher.
E. Run-in headings	E. <u>Legislative influences</u>. After the election, several factors influenced the legislative agenda. Most programs were reevaluated. The limited resources would now have to be distributed among several deserving causes.
F. Abbreviations	F. The retailer will meet the requirements of the C.D.I.
	The corner of Fourth St. and Elm Ave. is one of the busiest in town.
	Mr. and Mrs. Santiago will attend the reunion.

Fold out the Compact End Marks Summary in the back of the text-workbook so you can see it while you read the explanations and work on the exercises.

PERIODS

Periods rank second only to commas in frequency of use. We do not notice many uses of the period because they are so common.

A. Statements

Use the period to mark the end of a sentence.

We will go to town after lunch.

The need to develop an alternate approach will not be necessary until after the new budget is approved; however, we will not say that the circumstance will not change.

B. Commands

The command sentence (sometimes called an imperative sentence) also ends with a period.

Finish the rest of the job.

This sentence has an understood subject, the word *you*. If the command is especially strong, the sentence could end with an exclamation mark. (See Rule 3.) These sentences are often very short and have an understood subject.

C. Lists

The third use for the period is with a displayed list of numbered or lettered items. A period should follow each of the numbers or letters. These periods set off the numbers or letters from the items themselves. Here are some examples.

After we repay the loan, we will tackle these goals:
1. Additional staffing
2. New shelving
3. Additional advertising

The commission issued the following recommendations:
a. Increased funds for housing
b. Easier application procedures
c. More coordination between programs

If the items are complete sentences, then end each with a period.

D. Decimals

When periods are used with numbers they are called *decimals* to mark the difference between fractions and whole numbers and between dollars and cents.

After his research Marty found that the old gold coin was worth $285.50, an increase of 2.5 percent.

E. Run-in headings

The period can also be a way to mark a paragraph title. This is called a *run-in heading*. The period separates the run-in heading from the regular text of the paragraph. Although the run-in heading is not a sentence, it does have a period at the end. Look at this example and the one in the Compact End Marks Summary.

> <u>The coach's dilemma</u>. Coaches are always faced with the problem of which player to put in which positions. This crucial question can often be the difference between strong and weak teams. The coach must match the skills and talents of players to the skills needed for particular positions. The coach must balance the available players so alternate combinations are possible when players have injuries.

F. Abbreviations

A very important use of the period is to mark abbreviations. Some abbreviations have periods, and other abbreviations like the two-letter postal abbreviations for states have the periods deleted.

The best rule is to consult a recent dictionary or style book for the best use of periods with abbreviations. Know where to find the lists that reflect current uses.

SUMMARY

The period is the most commonly used end mark, ending most of our written sentences and separating many items for clarity. It separates fractional parts of numbers and money amounts. The period is also used as a separator to prevent readers from getting confused or lost with abbreviations. Use it accurately.

EXERCISE 1

RULE 1

Chapter 8   *END MARKS*

- Insert periods in the following examples and write the rule number and letter from the Compact End Marks Summary above each period you insert.
- The uses involve only periods.

Example: The report will be completed by the end of the week .^{1A}

1. Please make sure that your forms are complete

2. The supplies account in next year's budget will need only a slight increase of 2 1 percent

3. Be sureto make the following preparations for the test:
   1 Study the material thoroughly
   2 Rest well the night before
   3 Bring sharp pencils

4. <u>Important factors</u> Historians have discussed the causes of the Civil War in the United States for many years Although they mention many factors, most agree on the economic forces that separated the North and South

5. Mr and Mrs Williams will participate in the panel discussion

6. He left his new address: 4144 E Jefferson Rd , Huntsville, VA 12211

7. Sylvia, please arrange for the transportation to the convention

8. James T Wilson completed the final statistics of the study using a computer program from the university

9. I have not agreed with the recommendation for the following reasons:
   a No funds
   b No time
   c No available people

10. You will find that the captain has all of the necessary information

11. The test will use the oldest of the patterns

12. Even though cases of the new adhesive will weigh over 300 lbs , we can ship them overnight

13. We can still make a profit with costs that are 113 percent higher, but the prices will have to be stable

14. My greatest fear is that we will run out of time before we can get the project finished

15. Alan Lumowski, M D, will be the speaker at the monthly meeting

The answers are in the back of the text-workbook.

QUESTION MARKS
Chapter 8   *END MARKS*

LEARNING OBJECTIVES

After your study of End Marks Rule 2, you will be able to:
* Insert question marks correctly in question situations.
* Label question mark uses to show which type of question mark to use.

RULE 2: Use QUESTION MARKS to end a question or show doubt about a fact.

A. Direct question

B. Editorial meaning
   (only as a last resort for clarification)

A. Will that be all you need?

B. We cannot locate the additional 321 (?)
   registration forms.

Fold out the Compact End Marks Summary in the back of the text-workbook so you can see it while you read the explanations and work on the exercises.

QUESTION MARKS

The primary use of the question mark is the ending of a question, but it also can be used editorially. Although it is not used often, it is a useful mark for variety and a necessary mark to show meaning.

A. Direct questions

The sentences that are questions should be ended with question marks. Although we easily notice the question marks when they occur or when we write them, they are not used frequently. Question marks and exclamation marks make up less than five percent of the end marks used in writing.

Usually a question is made by changing the word order of a statement, but a question can be made out of a statement by simply changing the mark at the end of the sentence.

You are the leader here?

This sentence expresses the speaker's disbelief about the truth of the statement. It can also express the speaker's surprise enough to question it. A statement can become a question in another way too. The statement can be followed by a comma and a couple of words questioning the statement. These are tag questions.

You will be making all the travel arrangements, won't you?

B. Editorial meaning

Occasionally the question mark can be included within parentheses in the sentence to show doubt or comment about a fact within a sentence.

She was born May 29, 1911(?), in Cleveland.

In this example there is some doubt about the year. The writer tells the reader about that doubt with the question mark. Remember that this is not a substitute for knowing the facts or writing clearly. Use this sparingly.

You may have some questions about where to place question marks with other punctuation. If the question is a quotation, put the question mark inside the quotation marks. If the question applies to an entire statement, then you should put the question mark outside the quotation marks to show that the question applies to the entire statement. These two examples demonstrate these methods.

Jake asked, "Has all of the food for the party been ordered?"

Did Lydia really say, "I will be moving next month"?

SUMMARY

Use question marks to let the reader know a question is involved. You can also let the reader know there is doubt about information in a sentence. Use the question mark for sentence variety. It can enhance your writing.

EXERCISE 2A
Chapter 8   *END MARKS*

RULE 2

- Insert question marks in the following examples and write the rule number and letter from the Compact End Marks Summary above each question mark you insert.
- All the uses involve Rule 2.

Example: Have you completed your tax return yet ?²ᴬ

1. What is the latest date that I can reserve a room and plane ticket

2. How will the new department be organized

3. Is this the only size seven dress in this beautiful blue

4. "You can't tell which one is older, can you" Theresa asked as she examined the antiques.

5. Will you be traveling during the holiday break

6. Most authorities agree that the original idea was developed in 1966 ( ).

7. William will be installed as president of the club next month, won't he

8. Will Carl Hopkins, the manager of the store, interview the new applicants

9. Did Millie really tell you, "No more carts were available "

10. He was born early this century; April 26 ( ), 1914.

The answers are in the back of the text-workbook.

EXERCISE 2B

RULES 1–2

Chapter 8   *END MARKS*

- Insert periods and question marks in the following examples and write the rule number and letter from the Compact End Marks Summary above each period or question mark you insert.
- All the uses involve Rules 1 or 2.

Example: When will you finish with the cleaning so I can paint ?^{2A}

1. Will you be attending the meeting Friday afternoon

2. The president of the club has the responsibility for conducting the meeting

3. Bring me that adjustable wrench

4. The price of the new radio will be $2999

5. When you have finished with the painting, complete these jobs:
   a Remove the trash in the garage
   b Sweep the garage
   c Mop the garage floor

6. How many pages have you read in that new book

7. The team finished the season with a winning record, but the coach was not satisfied

8. His mother inquired, "Will you help me with the dishes "

9. <u>Literature study</u> Many courses in American literature are organized around the major historical periods These courses are also organized around other topics such as authors or literature types In all cases the courses involve investigating the major authors and movements

10. The discovery of the artifacts at the ruins shift the date of occupancy to 1150 ( )

11. Joseph, do not turn on the other machine

12. "How will we find all of the books if we do not catalog them " the bookstore owner asked the new employee

13. If you drive along Miles Ave until you cross the bridge, you will see all the major sites

14. The soccer game ended with a score of 1 to 0 after playing two overtime periods

15. After Alicia passed the exam, she opened her office as a C P A and began her practice

The answers are in the back the text-workbook.

EXCLAMATION MARKS
Chapter 8   *END MARKS*

LEARNING OBJECTIVES

After your study of End Marks Rule 3, you will be able to:
• Insert exclamation marks correctly in sentences.
• Label exclamation marks uses to show which exclamation use is appropriate.

RULE 3: Use EXCLAMATION MARKS to end a sentence or interjection with strong feeling.

A. Sentence
B. Interjection

A. That concert was amazing!
B. Wow! No wonder everyone is talking about the new cars; they are really different.

Fold out the Compact End Marks Summary in the back of the text-workbook so you can see it while you read the explanations and work on the exercises.

EXCLAMATION MARK

The exclamation mark is another mark used instead of the period. The exclamation mark is reserved to show strong feeling.

A. End of sentences

Use an exclamation mark to mark the end of a sentence that shows shock, surprise, or wonder.

> What a ballgame! I can't believe we won.

> You really are remarkable!

> Thank you. I'm thrilled with the new patterns!

Show the reader you mean an exclamation by ending those sentences with exclamation marks.

B. Interjection

You can use an exclamation mark following the first word or phrase used as an interjection. For business and technical writing, however, you should not use them often. Here are some examples.

> Phew! We finished just in time.

> Wow! You completed every question correctly.

> Look Out! The brakes are overheating.

These exclamations are not grammatically connected to the balance of the sentence. They are expressions of wonder or amazement that often begin a more detailed statement. Also, the exclamation mark is placed inside quotation marks when the exclamation applies to the direct words of the speaker.

> "Ethan, stop pounding on the keyboard like that!" Craig shouted as the three-year-old played with the computer.

SUMMARY

Remember to use the exclamation mark sparingly. Excessive use can dull its impact. Use the exclamation to mark to distinguish statements of strong emotion and to follow interjections followed by a connected sentence.

EXERCISE 3A
Chapter 8   *END MARKS*

RULE 3

- Insert exclamation marks in the following examples and write the rule number and letter from the Compact End Marks Summary above each exclamation mark you insert.
- The uses involve only exclamation marks. Some may be correct as written.
- In some situations periods may already be used where there should be an exclamation mark. If necessary, change the periods.

Example: Janie, you did a fantastic job !³ᴬ

1. That was a great game.

2. You were great. Thanks so much.

3. Gosh Can anything else happen?

4. What is the point of your objection?

5. Help I'm dropping all these packages.

6. Attention Your commander has just entered.

7. Go to your room now.

8. I know you don't believe me, but he is the man I saw.

9. Hurray We finished the project.

10. Emi replied quickly, "You can't mean it."

The answers are in the back of the text-workbook.

EXERCISE 3B

RULES 1–3

Chapter 8   *END MARKS*

- Insert end marks in the following examples and write the rule number and letter from the Compact End Marks Summary above each end mark you insert.
- The uses involve all end marks. Some may be correct as written.
- In some situations periods or commas may already be used where there should be an exclamation mark or a question mark. If necessary, change them.

Example: Well, will this be the last trip?   *2A*

1. How right you are.

2. "We cannot have all of the workers on first shift," Pat, the manager, exclaimed.

3. We cannot believe that every task is complete, can we.

4. We will need the resources of the executive committee, won't we.

5. Is this the last of the forms we need to process.

6. Of the 320 ( ) applications how many are from Texas.

7. We will need all of the following items for the proposal:
   1 Cost estimates
   2 A clear schedule
   3 An explanation of the plan

8. Mr Smiley, will you help with the treasurer's report.

9. Whew That car came really close.

10. We cannot win if many of our players have injuries.

11. <u>City plans</u> The leaders of the community will plan and develop a new park system. With the help of many clubs and organizations the new parks will be ready by next summer. Cooperation will make it possible.

12. There you are, Ms Arnberry. Will there be anything else.

13. Just saying that the price is between $200 and $300 is not enough. Be specific and say the price is $23499

14. The new paving project will begin on Madison Ave next week.

15. Stop Don't touch the hot iron.

The answers are in the back of the text-workbook.

SOLUTIONS

SOLUTION TO EXERCISE 1
Chapter 1   *COMMA*

1. The tour guide was fluent in English,^1A French,^1A and German.

2. We will need excellent actors,^1B a skilled director,^1B and a willing stage crew to produce the play.

3. Lauren worked hard in her arithmetic class to understand the problem,^1B complete a solution,^1B and check her answer.

4. Your order for lumber,^1B electrical parts,^1A and roofing cannot be filled until next week.

5. You will have to take everything out,^1A sweep thoroughly,^1B and wash the floor when you clean the garage.

6. Careful reading,^1B clear class notes,^1B and thorough review can lead a student to a good test score.

7. An efficient secretary should be able to work quickly,^1A accurately,^1A and politely.

8. You must devote most of your time to the task,^1C you must take calculated risks,^1C and you must have the patience to see your plans through in order to build a financial empire.

9. We liked your suggestion,^1B the way you presented it,^1B and the cost savings it will provide.

10. Summer brought thoughts of swimming,^1A picnics,^1A and time away from school.

11. Miss Smith will not stand for any more editing mistakes,^1B feeble excuses,^1B or missed deadlines.

12. Our business plan must demonstrate a clear marketing strategy,^1B a realistic budget,^1B forecast and a plan to rent equipment.

13. The paper supply and the toner and the copier count must be checked each day. ^NONE

14. We are sorry to report that your car has a transmission leak,^1B a radiator leak,^1B and two leaking shock absorbers.

15. The printer must be completely disconnected,^1C it must be taken to the shop,^1C and it must be reconditioned with new parts.

SOLUTION TO EXERCISE 2A
Chapter 1   *COMMA*

1. My grandfather sent us a letter at Christmas,²ᴬ but we haven't heard from him since.

2. We can use a large hand truck,²ᴬ or we can rent a hydraulic lift.

3. The results of our last tests indicate no immediate problem; however,²ᴮ we should retest in six months as a double check.

4. Management finds your plan a feasible,²ᶜ effective solution to the problem.

5. Carl designed the helpful gadget; however,²ᴮ he does not have the business skills needed to develop an organized,²ᶜ successful marketing campaign.

6. The upper bracket of the shelf must be fastened first,²ᴬ and the aligning holes must be predrilled.

7. I cannot agree with your solution,²ᴬ yet I can agree with your analysis of the problem.

8. I do not like the author's stilted,²ᶜ arrogant style.

9. The supervisor must work skillfully with people,²ᴬ yet she must also know the operation well.

10. Thorough research will provide the information,²ᴬ and clear writing will make it useful to others.

11. You will have to get permission to operate the equipment,²ᴬ or someone will be assigned to operate it for you.

12. Mr. Baker can be a reasonable man when he gets enough sleep the previous night. *NONE*

13. Cathy raced to the stage to receive the award she had earned for her diligent,²ᶜ thorough work.

14. Sam's imagination ran wild,²ᴬ but no one paid attention when he spoke about his ideas.

15. A well-coached actor is able to deliver a confident,²ᶜ convincing dialect.

SOLUTION TO EXERCISE 2B
Chapter 1   *COMMA*

1. Streets,[1A] bridges,[1A] and railroad crossings were severely damaged during the storm.

2. Your conclusions must be based on complete data,[2A] yet I do not see enough figures to justify your answer.

3. A roving eye,[1B] an attentive ear,[1B] and continued patience will serve the inexperienced, anxious hunter well.

4. Charlie's well-developed imagination helped him as a writer,[2C][2A] but it did not solve his problems with grammar and spelling.

5. The missing pages in the ledger made the accounts an inadequate,[2C] incomplete record of last month's business.

6. The project is finally finished,[2A] and I have spent five busy,[2C] challenging years working on it.

7. Our security measures include hourly checks by guards,[1B] limited-access keys,[1B] and video monitoring.

8. Howard's humor is not always clear to the rest of us; however,[2B] he seems to have an enormous supply of quips, puns, and stories for all occasions.

9. As a sales representative I try to be personable and polite,[1A][1A][2A] but I also try to maintain a professional distance.

10. Several companies may be willing to pay for the market research if the information is clear, if the information is complete, and if the information is valid.[1C][1C]

11. Some supervisors will always be patient, yet others are often curt with everyone.

12. Often the most careful writer will make obvious,[2A][2C] unnecessary editing mistakes.

13. The new mansion will have distinctive features including a walk-in refrigerator and a round swimming pool. *NONE*

14. We will adopt the new procedure when we can get a new computer,[1C] when we can find the right software,[1C] and when we can find the right printer.

15. Ms. Tarner will help us with the project now,[2A] but we will still need more time to work on it this summer.

SOLUTION TO EXERCISE 3A
Chapter 1   *COMMA*

1. Elmer,^{3A} I told you we could not fix that now.

2. In conclusion,^{3H} the most difficult tasks are behind us.

3. If these pages are not printed by Friday,^{3F} the report will not be mailed on time.

4. Standing on the diving platform,^{3D} the Olympic diver prepared for her last dive in the series.

5. Yes,^{3B} you may go to the movie later this afternoon.

6. On the other hand,^{3H} you may have a good point.

7. In a case with several problems without answers,^{3C} the researchers must clarify the specific questions.

8. Dashing toward his waiting spaceship,^{3D} Buck Rogers fired at the approaching aliens.

9. After you have connected the retainer,^{3F} you must inspect it for a good fit.

10. Determined to make a good first impression,^{3D} Ana Maria headed from the parking lot toward her new job.

11. To gather all the information,^{3E} I will need to write several letters to many of our major customers.

12. Because the race was close,^{3F} the official announcement of the winner was delayed for half an hour.

13. The engine humming at idle,^{3G} the convertible was parked at the curbside while the campers were in the convenience store.

14. Carmella will be ready to depart at 7:00 a.m. *NONE*

15. With all of the patents on past inventions,^{3C} I sometimes wonder how new items are even registered.

SOLUTION TO EXERCISE 3B
Chapter 1   *COMMA*

1. Scurrying to finish before the bell rang, *3D* the students in cooking class cleaned the counters, *3A* replaced the pots and pans, *1B* and washed the dishes in record time.

2. Gloria, *3A 1B* I told you that I did not want you to alter the schedule, *2A* but I guess we can live with it now that the changes have been made.

3. If you do not like the way we do things around here, *3F* you can leave; and you should take your grumbling, *2C* sarcastic friend with you.

4. In summary, *3H* your current operation is not large enough for additional employees; but a small computer, *1B* an accounting software package, *1B* and a word processing software package can increase the current employees' productivity.

5. Our final plans include an advertising campaign, *1B* a benefit dance, *1B* and 5,000 direct mail flyers.

6. We found the new clerk to be a well-mannered, *2C* considerate person.

7. Meeting in secret for over three months, *3D* the management of the company arranged for its merger.

8. Some employees find the work challenging, *1A* rewarding, *1A* and entertaining.

9. Oh, *3B* I did not realize that you wanted to register for the class also.

10. Mr. Jones, *3A* we hope that your order reaches you in time for the sale, *2A* and we also hope that your new building will serve your growing company.

11. As the car coasted slowly to a stop, *3F* the driver and passengers groaned in unison.

12. The report must include the cost, *1A* price, *1A* and quantity of each item on the order along with a concise, *2C* clear description of the item.

13. The fire destroyed twenty of the thirty apartments in the building; no one was injured. *NONE*

14. When the invoice is processed in our office, *3F* we record all the amounts, *1B* note the supplier's address, *1B* and send the invoice to the accounts payable department.

15. Although you may not want to study the complicated, *2C* detailed reports, *3F* someone must make the decision.

SOLUTION TO EXERCISE 4A
Chapter 1   *COMMA*

1. With proper care,[4A] Mrs. Phillips,[4A] your new car should last well past 100,000 miles.

2. The chairs,[4C] not the table,[4C] must be moved first.

3. A careful study of our catalog,[4D] provided for you at no cost,[4D] will detail our complete product line.

4. The dealer will also provide financing and insurance for your new car,[4B] a sports model with a sunroof.

5. The newest version of the program,[4E] which was published last month,[4E] has all of the revisions you requested.

6. Careful planning will,[4G] I believe,[4G] solve many of the problems associated with the new computer application.

7. Jack Naife,[4B] the president of the local bank,[4B] was just elected mayor.

8. The sales manager will consider all of your offers,[4E] which are provided in our contract proposal.

9. The letter will be provided after the contract is signed,[4G] i.e.,[4G] after the agreement is official.

10. The protective cover,[4D] mounted over the delicate connections,[4D] is made of a heat-resistant material.

11. Most of the accounting problems,[4E] which cannot be solved with a better calculator, must be resolved through a close examination of the receipts. [4E]

12. Ms. Susan Harper,[4B] the vice president of finance for the company,[4B] will be presenting the annual report during the meeting.

13. You will find that your study of the text will be most helpful when you take this test. *NONE*

14. James Cotter,[4E] who is a consultant for both business and government office operations, will provide us with a clearer picture of all the decision factors. [4E]

15. We cannot approve your application at this time; we will reconsider it in six months, however. [4G]

SOLUTION TO EXERCISE 4B
Chapter 1   *COMMA*

1. Our club president will, *[4G]* no doubt, *[4G]* finish the project; and he will then turn over the office to another ambitious, aspiring leader.

2. Visiting the hospital with her Aunt Jane, *[2C]* Tina became interested in volunteer work herself. *[3D]*

3. Our new model offers many advantages over our competition and our older model, *[4G]* e.g. , *[4G]* lower initial costs, higher efficiency, *[1B]* and a longer time between scheduled maintenance checks. *[1B]*

4. Billy, *[3A]* you need to apply another coat of paint to the doghouse, *[2A]* but you will have to wait until we get more paint, however.

5. Our goals and accomplishments, *[4G]* *[4C]* not our fears and disappointments, *[4C]* must govern our feelings of self-worth.

6. Those unfamiliar abbreviations, *[4B]* a shortcut you use, *[4B]* are very confusing for people who do not know them.

7. After the purchasing agent completes the requisition, *[3F]* the order is immediately forwarded, but you may not get the receipt for a few days.

8. Yes, *[3B]* *[2A]* I think your plan will provide the advantage we need, *[4B]* faster delivery time.

9. On the other hand, *[3H]* we cannot ignore the new products provided by our innovative, *[2C]* aggressive competitors.

10. John Steinbeck, *[4E]* who is a famous writer most of us have encountered in school, *[4E]* had many critics in his early years.

11. If you follow all of the steps, *[3F]* you will be able to assemble the unit without a technician.

12. Without thinking about all the consequences of his actions, *[3C]* the rodeo cowboy mounted the bronco and nodded for the gate to open.

13. The leader will need to show a solid plan, *[1B]* a willingness to talk about it, *[1B]* and the perseverance to repeat it several times.

14. Professor Davis will verify the calculations. *NONE*

15. Tom Hector, *[4B]* the author of the novel, *[4B]* used the first three chapters to develop the situation and the characters, a group of race car drivers. *[4B]*

SOLUTION TO EXERCISE 5A
Chapter 1   *COMMA*

1. He will have to move to Chicago,⁵ᴬ Illinois,⁵ᴬ to accept the new job.

2. This is the last row of weeds,⁵ᴴ isn't it?

3. My aunt said,⁵ᶜ "Please come back for another visit soon."

4. Robert Tanaka,⁵ᶠ M.D.,⁵ᶠ will be the president of the association next year.

5. Dear Uncle Henry,⁵ᴱ

   Thank you for the graduation gift. I plan to use it next year in college.

   Your youngest nephew,⁵ᴱ
   Tom

6. The Declaration of Independence was signed on July 4,⁵ᴮ 1776.

7. Dear Mr. Carlson:

   Your order will be processed immediately. We apologize for the delay.

   Sincerely,⁵ᴰ
   Manuel Ramos,⁴ᴮ Sales Manager

8. The report indicates sales of 104,⁵ᴵ 855 units last month.

9. "This practice should be stopped before the next court session,⁵ᶜ" the judge declared.

10. The members of the committee included:

    Hayes,⁵ᴳ Jeffrey
    Hollingshead,⁵ᴳ Alison
    Schneider, Candy

11. Dear Mr. Jones:⁵ᴳ

    Please consider my application for department clerk.

    Sincerely,⁵ᴰ
    Amy Smith

12. We left our car in Houston,⁵ᴬ Texas,⁵ᴬ with a damaged engine.

13. The most difficult problem was solved when the leaders from Portland,⁵ᴬ Oregon,⁵ᴬ signed a new agreement on August 12,⁵ᴬ 1974.

14. Several cities were cited in 19—⁵ᴮ as outstanding for their work with new schools. *NONE*

15. Beth Wilson,⁵ᶠ Ph.D.,⁵ᶠ spoke at the meeting on October,⁵ᴮ 2 19—.

SOLUTION TO EXERCISE 5B
Chapter 1   *COMMA*

1. After we complete this project,[3F] we will all have to find new jobs.

2. Running to catch the departing airliner,[3D] the passenger dropped his luggage tag with his destination,[4B] Cincinnati,[5A] Ohio.

3. Tracy,[3A] please stop saying,[5A] "I don't want to go."

4. His offbeat opinions,[4C] not his political opponents,[5C][4C] contributed to his loss in the recent election.

5. The judge will,[4G] no doubt,[4G] make her ruling later in the week,[2A] but the implications of it may last for several years.

6. The meeting was held in Newark,[5A] New Jersey,[5A] on October 23,[5B] 1976,[5B] to discuss the final details of the contract.

7. In conclusion,[3H] let me say that I have enjoyed your pleasant,[2C] congenial company.

8. Arthur Critick,[4B] the journalist responsible for the article,[4B] refused to reveal his sources.

9. We hope for excellent results from our goals for next quarter; i.e.,[4G] we hope to increase productivity by 10 percent,[1B] expand to two new markets,[1B] and maintain low overhead costs.

10. The president of the humane society,[4E] whom we all recognize as a fair person,[4E] will make the final selection of an assistant manager.

11. The backers of the plan will require additional political support for the plan to have a chance. *NONE*

12. "If the most qualified candidates are chosen,[3F] we will have a well-balanced department,"[5C] the chief indicated in the interview.

13. We will use block construction,[4C] not frame walls,[4C] for the three remaining new houses in this developed,[2C] older neighborhood.

14. You were able to complete the problems,[2A] but your answers were not accurate.

15. The letter was mailed to your address in Atlanta,[5A] Georgia,[5A] after you moved on July 12,[5B] 19—.

SOLUTION TO EXERCISE 5C
Chapter 1   *COMMA*

Peterson's Plastics
1089 East Juniper Lane
Logan, UT 84321
      5'A
            5B
January 13, 19—

               4B
Mr. Phil Snidley, President
Phamous Manufacturing
1111 West Cedar Drive
Davis, CA 95616
      5'A

Dear Mr. Snidley:

                                    2A
We have reviewed your proposal, but our evaluation team has
                        3H
rejected it. In summary, your proposal attacks the basic prob-
    2A
lem, yet it neglects the practical matters associated with
implementing the solution. You do not provide financial guide-
      1B   *1B*
lines, a realistic time frame, or a staffing estimate. With
                          4A   *4A*
your record of success, Mr. Snidley, we are somewhat disappointed.

                                                3F
    If you care to revise your final offer, please send it by
          5B   *5B*   *5A*   *5A*
January 31, 19—, to 234 Eastern Avenue, Pasadena CA, 91107. We
                                    4E
cannot accept it after that date, which is based on other cor-
                                        5H
porate obligations. The extra work is worthwhile, isn't it?

          5D
Sincerely,

               4B
Mrs. Sally King, Purchasing Agent

194

SOLUTION TO EXERCISE 5D
Chapter 1   *COMMA*

MEMORANDUM

TO:	Bill Diamond
FROM:	Clover Needhap
DATE:	April 7,^5B 19—
SUBJECT:	AB1 400 Evaluation Report

In summary,^3H the AB1 400 unit is a quick,^2C reliable device; however,^2B we are not happy with its price. Although we found some problems with the documentation,^3F all were easily overcome with only minor revisions. The accompanying interface,^4D included at no extra cost,^4D makes the system complete. The printer,^1A the interface,^1A and the unit are all available from Cactus Computer Connections,^5A 1414 East Thirsty Circle,^5A Death Valley,^5A California 92328. If you need additional information,^3F give me a call on Extension 667.

SOLUTION TO EXERCISE 1
Chapter 2   *SEMICOLON*

1. The order for Carlson Manufacturing is complete; **1B** however, we cannot ship it until tomorrow.

2. All the fines have been; **1A** paid your record is clear.

3. The conference call was cancelled; **1B** therefore, we will also have to reschedule our planning meeting.

4. The handful of members at the meeting decided on the plan; **1A** we all must now support it.

5. Our approach to the problem is more methodical; **1B** however, we will still need a little inspiration.

6. Mr. Katz, the paper you submitted is acceptable; **1B** however, you may wish to expand it later.

7. The sample illustrates the problem; **1A** it does not confirm your proposed solution.

8. You will have several chances; **1B** nevertheless, every one must be a wholehearted effort.

9. Glorious clouds swirled in the sky; **1A** we watched in awe from the protection of the porch.

10. You can redeem the coupon; **1B** however, you must make the purchase with cash.

11. My disorganized attempt to gather a consensus failed; **1A** I will be more organized next time.

12. The 30-second commercial was scheduled for a time slot following the evening news; therefore, the slot before the news is available. **1B**

13. Randall ran the race with the world record as his goal; **1A** he failed to achieve it.

14. With a bold gesture the chairperson allowed one more motion; **1B** however, that one motion called for two hours of debate.

15. You may be certain that the rules will always apply, yet they are not always enforced. **NONE**

SOLUTION TO EXERCISE 2A
Chapter 2 *SEMICOLON*

1. If you do not feel like a competent, confident leader, you will not show leadership to others; yet those others will look for someone's lead to follow.
   2B

2. We will need to confirm reservations in all of the listed cities: Chicago, Illinois; Pittsburg, Pennsylvania; and Newark, New Jersey.
   2A

3. We cannot always recognize, control, or eliminate the fear of public speaking; yet we can write in a protected, private environment.
   2A   *2B*

4. Before we begin the project we must interview Sam Dillion, the finance manager; Susan Castillo, the director of marketing; and Charles Aiken, the retired planning manager.
   2A   *2A*

5. During his first one hundred days in office President Franklin D. Roosevelt made several bold moves: he changed the way people looked at government work; he spoke to the people directly about the problems; and he demanded support from Congress.
   2C   *2C*

6. Although we have made our selection for this supervisory position, you will find that other opportunities will soon be available; yet you must compete with other capable, experienced individuals.
   2B

7. For warranty service the following conditions are required: authorized factory dealers must complete the repairs; you must insure shipping; and you must complete the registration.
   2C   *2C*

8. On May 18, 1992, the manager completed the overbudget, overdue project; but the months of effort exhausted him.
   2B

9. Jim will find the only way is to make changes: he will have to promote the right people; he will have to select new people who will get results; and he will need to set some clear goals for them to pursue.
   2C   *2C*

10. The computer and printer were thoroughly tested: we ran the software with sample data; we printed all twelve of the reports; and we rechecked a sample of the calculations by hand.
    2C   *2C*

11. My reservations about the proposal involve the required labor hours, the details of the maintenance agreement, and the need for an alternate power source. *NONE*

12. If you are awarded the contract, Miss Davis, you will need to refurbish the old building, which is in an older district; plan for new highway access, which also will be an expensive aspect of the project; and develop an acceptable schedule.
    2A   *2A*

SOLUTION TO EXERCISE 2B
Chapter 2   *SEMICOLON*

1. Patient strength can overcome doubt; *1A* impatient anger may force the wrong action.

2. Older methods have proven themselves through the test of time; *1B* however, innovation can make them more efficient.

3. For an alternate site you could consider these cities: Boston, Massachusetts; *2A* Atlanta, Georgia; *2A* or Charleston, South Carolina.

4. We can make the needed changes in the plan; *1B* however, the date the project is finished will also change.

5. The physician moved quietly through the rooms and halls as she made her morning rounds; *1A* all patients were making progress.

6. Masterfully compiling statistic after statistic, the baseball announcer prepared for the playoff game; *1B* therefore, when the team was ready to take the field, he spoke to the radio listeners with authority about the team's history.

7. With the prototypes of his invention firmly in hand, Calvin began the process of testing including a variety of tests: electromagnetic interference to make sure it would not cause problems with neighbors; *2C* cold temperature operation to make certain that it would work in the cold winters of Minnesota; *2C* and endurance tests to determine how long it would actually last in operation.

8. Proper accounting methods can solve many financial problems of a new business; *1A* no substitute will do.

9. The fascinating feature of the new building is the way that the elevator is visible from the outside and provides a beautiful view for the riders. *NONE*

10. A critical manufacturing process can be changed only when all the variables have been considered: the costs of new equipment and servicing it; *2C* the long-term facilities impact in terms of changes in square footage and associated mechanical changes; *2C* and labor impact including not only the time involved but the fatigue of workers.

11. We will not develop the alternate plan now; *1B* therefore, the need for an additional building and office space is not necessary.

12. Another way of looking at the problem, Ms. Smiley, is that we can meet all your requirements without any additional cost; *2B* but you must agree to allow some flexibility in your demanding, accelerated schedule.

SOLUTION TO EXERCISE 3A
Chapter 2   *SEMICOLON*

1. The concerns for our meeting *3B*; i.e., the budget for next year and the schedule for projects, must be discussed thoroughly before we make the final decisions.

2. Several of the reasons we approved the purchase *3B*; that is, the advantages we saw at the time, have not shown actual improvement in operation.

3. You may cover all the material in your presentation *3B*; that is, you may even cover the material that is normally only shown to your department.

4. When the mistakes are obvious *3A*; e.g., missing letters, incorrect spacing, or crooked text, both the editor and the printer are at fault.

5. Patience with the new computer program in the face of frustration *3B*; that is, waiting until your skill matches your desire for the program to work, will serve you in the long run.

6. To become even reasonably proficient, beginning tennis players must work on several skills at the same time; i.e., serving, volleying, forehand strokes, and backhand strokes.

7. No complaints will be aired *3B* at the meeting *3B*; that is, they will not be discussed openly.

8. All along the trail the hikers found evidence of many people using the trail *3A*; i.e., paper litter, beverage cans, and a well-worn path with no vegetation.

9. You will probably not find any software that is available for that outdated computer model. *NONE*

10. You may not use statistical techniques that are unfamiliar to your novice audience; e.g., standard deviation, margin of error, and degree of confidence.   *3A*

SOLUTION TO EXERCISE 3B
Chapter 2   *SEMICOLON*

1. If you do not complete the project on time, your supervisor will not be pleased *1B*; however, the customer will accept a delayed delivery.

2. The district sales offices will be moved to San Francisco, California *2A*; St. Louis, Missouri *2A*; and Newark, New Jersey.

3. Later in the month we will be conducting a complete inventory *3B*; i.e., we will count the stock in every storage bin and workstation.

4. Many students find math a difficult subject *1A*; others find it fascinating and learn easily.

5. All of the following alterations will be made before the end of the month: the storage racks will be moved *2C*; the new lighting will be installed *2C*; and the furniture will be replaced.

6. Businesses use a variety of advertising media including magazines, TV, and radio *2A*; but their results vary because they target dramatically different markets.

7. We must complete all of the preparations for the meeting *3B*; that is, we must be ready with a complete agenda and adequate facilities.

8. The data you requested confirm the conclusion *1B*; moreover, the report adds enough information that others can study the problem.

9. Historically the president has served as a balance of power to the other branches *1B*; however, in today's environment these traditional roles have changed.

10. The total shipment is ready *3B*; that is, the inspections are complete and the units are packaged in their crates.

11. Metric units of measure will be used for the projected development of the new space probe *3B*; namely, all specifications and requirements will use these units.

12. Proofreaders will not like the newer system of marking the copy because it will not use symbols with which they are familiar. *NONE*

13. We will hold a conference with the following main officers: Carl Pastor, director of marketing *2A*; Samantha Colter, vice president of sales *2A*; and Susan Talmut, director of public relations.

14. How will we answer the budget questions *3B*; i.e., what will be our rationale for the requests?

15. Coach Johnson is losing his patience *1A*; he is beginning to pace on the sidelines.

SOLUTION TO EXERCISE 1

Chapter 3   *COLON*

1. We will not be able to attend the meeting tomorrow at 3 :15 p.m. *1A*

2. While he was in Europe, Frank Pastor wrote the book *George Patton :General and Leader.* *1C*

3. The Reds outscored the Mets during the season 3 :2. *1D*

4. The minister took her sermon from Mark 4 :23. *1B*

5. The leader of the group began the study series, *Job's Troubles :A Perspective for Troubled Times,* with a look at the first section of chapter one, Job 1 :1–23. *1C* *1B*

6. Without complete cooperation we will not get done before the deadline, which is your meeting at 2 :30 p.m. *1B*

7. The radio announcer completed the program, "We'll have more music until the hour of three." *NONE* *1A*

8. Although the community leaders were working hard, they were not able to change the voter registration beyond the 5 :1 proportion of eligible voters to registered ones. *1D*

9. The parable of the Good Samaritan, to which she frequently referred, is in Luke 10 :30–37. *1B*

10. With great fanfare the publishers launched the new magazine, *Presents :Your Guide to Giftgiving.* *1C*

SOLUTION TO EXERCISE 2A
Chapter 3   *COLON*

1. Resolved:[2B] The Symphony Support Organization (SSO) will provide half of the funding for the new concert hall.

2. Tammy:[2C]   Be sure to call when you get to the ranch.

   Thom:[2C]   OK, but it won't be before next week.

   Tammy:[2C]   Thanks, I'll wait for the call.

3. Madame Chairman and members of the board:[2A] I would like to nominate James Castle for next year's president.

4. Tina Barker:[2C]   No, I will not go with you unless you change your clothes first.

   Vinny Barker:[2C] Sure, just because you don't approve of the color of my shirt, I have to change it.

   TB:[2C]   It's not just me. That color is awful.

   VB:[2C]   Well, I like it.

5. Patterhoff, Patricia. *Open to the Public*. San Francisco:[2D] Porpoise Publishing, 1990.

6. We will now take a break before studying *Hamlet* III:[2D] ii.

7. Mr. President, Mr. Peters, friends, and family:[2A] you have selected me for this honor, and I thank you with all my heart.

8. Arthur:[2C]   We can't finish by the deadline!

   Pam:[2C]   We have to; the trucks won't wait.

9. Castle, Brenda. *Patience in the Face of Danger*. Newark:[2D] Alternative Press, 1993.

10. Delanty, Robert, "The Effects of Amino Acids on Digestion of Fructose," *Journal of Nutritional Science*, 1:[2D]12–55, November 1993.

SOLUTION TO EXERCISE 2B
Chapter 3   *COLON*

1. Resolved**:** *(2B)* The Library Development Board will establish a fund to assist with the acquisition of additional materials for student research.

2. Thomas**:** *(2C)*   We can't find the lost keys, Patty.

   Patty**:** *(2C)*   But you won't need them if the door is unlocked.

3. When Albert Frances spoke at the luncheon, he read from his new book *After the Gold Rush***:** *(1C)* *California History in the 1860's.*

4. Your odds of success are only 3**:**2 *(1D)*, which is not enough for a favorable vote.

5. Madame President, members of the club, and guests**:** *(2A)* I find it fitting that we should meet today near the location of this historical event.

6. Kathy, the bus will depart promptly at 7**:**30 *(1A)* a.m.; the driver will not wait.

7. Killjoy, Francine. "Older Americans Find Happiness," *The Reporter,* 23**:** *(2D)* 55–59.

8. Resolved**:** *(2B)* The members of the executive committee will vote to approve the content of the annual report which will be titled *Lifeline***:** *(1C)* *A Report to the Hospital Shareholders.*

9. We will not wait past 6**:**30 *(1A)* p.m. for her to return from the errand. *(1C)*

10. Mr. Chairman, fellow delegates, and visiting students**:** *(2A)* Making a speech this evening will not complete my assignment; it will only serve . . .

11. BK**:** *(2C)*   Hold it! Our payroll is in that strongbox.

    TG**:** *(2C)*   Too bad. Hand it over anyway.

12. Our chances of finishing the project by the deadline are only 4**:**1 *(1D)*.

13. After the priest began the lesson everyone knew he was talking about John 3**:**16 *(1B)*.

14. You can find the information in the bibliography.

    Paquette, William. *All is Will.* New York **:** *(2D)* Dieters Publishing, Inc., 1989.

15. As members of the delegation and guests, we are entitled to hear the additonal remarks of the speaker without an additional fee. *NONE*

SOLUTION TO EXERCISE 3A
Chapter 3   *COLON*

1.   To:*3D* Carl Samson
    From:*3D* Sally Alvarez
    Date:*3D* 3/7/--
    Subject: Vacation Schedule
         3D

    Since summer is just around the corner, please have everyone in your department mark the schedule with planned vacations . . .

2. Dear Mrs. Castle:*3B*

    Thank you for your order No. 9726. It was shipped on Thursday, March 2. Please let me know if you have not received the merchandise by March 15.

    Sincerely,

    Chris Battel

3. Dear Dr. Caplet:*3B*

    You are cordially invited to the annual meeting of the fellows of Old Main. We will be celebrating our 100th anniversary this year. Please bring old photos.

    Cordially,

    Sam J. Jones

    SJJ: krg
       1A
4. Dear Mr. Jacobs:*3B*

    Subject:*3E* Order Number 12389 dated 7/6/--

    We have been able to locate only three of the items you ordered. The other two, the special edition of Dickens' *A Christmas Carol* and the pamphlet on the Constitution, are not available at this time. Please let us know if you want to postpone or cancel the order.

    Respectfully,

    Jason Sabor

5. Dear Captain Barnes: *3B*

The oldest record of inspection of the house at 123 South Elm Drive is dated June 14, 1968. Although we have searched for further evidence of insurance coverage prior to that date, we do not have any other older records available. We hope this information is helpful in your investigation of the fire. We are obliged to let Miss Reams, the owner, know of your inquiry.

Sincerely,

Becky Stone

cc: *3C* Andrea Reams

6.   To: *3D* Jason Badder
      From: *3D* Samuel Oldcastle
      Date: *3D* 4/17/--
   Subject: New policy for travel requests
            3D

Because the budget for corporate travel is limited until the end of the year, all requests must be approved at least ten days in advance. This will allow for proper balancing between territories needing service. Thanks for your cooperation.

7. Dear Ms. Sanchez: *3B*

You will find that the enclosed information will help you determine which model you would like to order. If we can be of further help, please let us know.

Sincerely,

Keith Hammond

KH: *3A* jjk

8. Dear Aunt Hilda,

I'm sorry I was late with your birthday gift. Bill was traveling, and the kids kept me busy. We hope to visit on the 3rd of next month. Let me know if that is okay.

Love,

Karen *NONE*

SOLUTION TO EXERCISE 3B
Chapter 3   *COLON*

1. Resolved *2B*: The Environmental Impact Committee will commission a study of the proposed construction and fund the study from its own resources.

2. The poet read from his latest collection *Rhymes Without Reasons*: *Poems of a Playful Mind.*

3. Mandrake, James R., "The Oldest Veteran," *Historical Journal*, 112 *1C*: 22 *2D*, August 1993.

4. Bob: *2C*   Why do you always second guess what I want to say?

   Melanie: *2C*   You know I don't mean to.

   Bob: *2C*   Well, it still bothers me, so try to quit.

5. Mr. Chairman, members of the board, and fellow delegates: *2A* I hope you will forgive the change of agenda. We want to begin this evening with a number of business items and then move on to our featured speaker.

6. Dear Mr. Perez: *3B*

   We will not be able to attend the convention this year. Although we have found it valuable in the past, the budget this year does not allow travel. We hope to return the following year. I will also notify Bill Johnson, the accommodations coordinator.

   Sincerely,

   Frank Skyler

   cc: *3C* Bill Johnson

7. The parable of the Good Samaritan is found at Luke 10 *1B*: 30–37.

8. Jones, Elmer. *Healthy Nutrition for Everyone*. Philadelphia: Nostar Publishing Company, 1993.

9. You will find that a proportion of 5 to 7 is the best for the *2D* team and the individual. *NONE*

10. Dear Ms. Sanger: *3B*

    Subject: *3E* Questions on Invoice #5677

    Although your invoice arrived promptly, we have enough questions that we must delay payment until the answers are clear.

    Is the first figure in column 3 the total for all items or only for those shipped?

    Does the billing for freight include the items shipped under the second delayed delivery?

    If you can answer these questions, we can clarify the amount due and get the payment to you.

    Sincerely,

    Della Jones

    pc: *3C* Allison Walton, Accounts Payable

SOLUTION TO EXERCISE 4A
Chapter 3   *COLON*

1. We will need the following to begin the cleanup project *4A* :

   - Volunteers
   - Transportation
   - Permits

2. You will find that I don't care about written plans *4F* : your evaluation depends on results.

3. We never fool ourselves *4F* : we only try to fool others.

4. Please add the following to your list of concerns *4A* :

   - Adequate budget
   - Sufficient resources
   - Clearly defined schedule

5. Note *4E* : the completed reports will be available after the first of the week.

6. In all of his former positions he cared primarily about his bosses' concerns *4D* : profits.

7. We will find that the main point can be summarized in Martin's latest remark *4B* :

   The golden age of the large corporation is behind us. From now on we will see the emergence of the smaller, more responsive organization.

8. As we finish the environmental project, be sure to complete the following tests *4A* : air quality, water quality, and noise impact.

9. She felt that this was the main problem in providing an adequate solution to the problem : *4C* all of the major opponents had different alternatives upon which they could not agree.

10. The final implementation will take several months because the details will not be completed as quickly as we originally planned. *NONE*

SOLUTION TO EXERCISE 4B
Chapter 3   *COLON*

1. The minister lead the service with a passage from James 4 *1B* :12–15.

2. Our proposal will need to meet all of the requirements *4A* : sufficient staff, adequate manufacturing facilities, and adequate transportation alternatives.

3. For the party we will have to arrange for the following *4A* :

    - Entertainment
    - Food
    - Doorprizes

4. As the planned changes take effect, we will notice the following *4A* :

    - Improved customer relations
    - Better profit margins
    - More productive employees

5. The plane will be departing from Gate 17 at 6 *1A* :45 a.m.

6. Dear Dr. Marshall *:3B*

    The information you requested is included in the reprints I have enclosed. I hope you find them valuable. If I can be of further service, please call us at 1-800-555-3456.

    Sincerely,

    Carl Wohl

7. Caution *4E* : the cover plate must be secured before starting the unit or electric shock may occur.

8. Please note that the following items are required for our new customer's kit *4A* :

    - Additional order forms
    - Warranty registration
    - Service center telephone numbers

9.   To: *3D* Cassie Lowery
        From: *3D* Carl Faberg
         Date: *3D* 3/3/--
      Subject: *3D* Next year's budget request

    Be sure to send the figures to me by Friday. In addition, we will . . .

10. Maybe I can finish this soon *4F* : there are more ways than one to solve a problem.

SOLUTION TO EXERCISE 4B (continued)

11. Mr. Chairman, Madame President, and members of the board: *2A* as you can imagine I am highly honored to receive this award. Your interest in my work has been a personally satisfying return for the effort.

12. Ester: *2C*   We will have to make the best of the situation.

    Tom: *2C*   I know, but you'll have to help me.

13. In summary, the new staff will be faced with several problems such as low worker morale, tight budgets, and a significant backlog of work. *NONE*

14. The last thing the author wrote was the title of the book which was *Personal Growth*: *How to Change Your Habits*. *1C*

15. The biggest problem facing the new manager was that the return rate exceeded the sales rate by a ratio of 3: 2. *1D*

SOLUTION TO EXERCISE 1
Chapter 4   *APOSTROPHE*

1. church

church	churches
church's	churches'

2. aunt

aunt	aunts
aunt's	aunts'

3. job

job	jobs
job's	jobs'

4. The film's title reflected the directors thinking. It was *All My Trials*.
    1A,

5. The runner's best effort was not enough to win the race.
    1A,

6. My report will not meet the boss's expectations.
    1A,

7. The twins will need more attention. Now the babies' needs are met by two people.
    1B,

8. The varying notches will make the keys' comparison difficult.
    1B,

9. The keeper asked, "How will we remodel the monkeys' cage? We have no place for them."
    1B,

10. The women's organization will meet more regularly after their organizational meetings are complete.
    1B,

11. Yesterday's results will be reported in tomorrow's newspaper.
    1A,   *1A,*

12. I doubt his conscience will let him forget. *NONE*

13. We will not be able to finish the project on time even with the three weeks' study we have devoted.
    1B,

14. The shopper asked the clerk for directions to the children's department.
    1B,

15. The police investigated the robbery at Jones' Garage.
    1A,

SOLUTION TO EXERCISE 2A
Chapter 4   *APOSTROPHE*

1. We can[2B]'t seem to find all of the books you[2B]'ve ordered.

2. "If you insist, we[2B]'ll start doin[2C]' it your way."

3. Why won[2B]'t she listen to my ideas?

4. The champion KO[2D]'d the challenger in the third round.

5. The guards will find that the monitor isn[2B]'t in its old location.

6. I[2B]'ll take care of the telephone order if you[2B]'ll finish the log book.

7. We can[2B]'t complete your order until you give us all of the instructions.

8. We may find that although the manager ok[2D]'d the request, it was not completed correctly.

9. "If you[2B]'re not ready, we may be startin[2C]' without you."

10. Her note read, "Cancel the nat[2B]'l meeting."

11. "That[2B]'ll cost us even if we can get past the initial problem."

12. Maybe the older of the dogs will teach the younger one by example. *NONE*

13. I remember that we had a much better team in [2A]'88 than in [2A]'89.

14. The coldest weather will cause the most damage to the crop; don[2B]'t you agree?

15. The experienced editors will complete the manuscript even though they won[2B]'t have all the final artwork for another month.

SOLUTION TO EXERCISE 2B
Chapter 4   *APOSTROPHE*

1. All instructors should attend at least one leader ^1B^'s conference.

2. "We can ^2B^'t find all of the answers. Are you goin ^2C^' to help?"

3. fox

fox	foxes
fox's	foxes'

4. How can we observe those pigeons ^1B^' nesting activities?

5. The oldest characters in the play will have to have two weeks ^1B^' growth of beard.

6. "Samuel, I know we filed the application forms in ^2A^'88."

7. child

child	children
child's	children's

8. "Has the boss ok ^2D^'d the purchase order yet?"

9. "I ^2B^'m sure your leavin ^2C^' will hurt his feelings."

10. The waiters will be serving the desert after the speaker ^1A^'s message.

11. The plan for a pilot project must be scrapped because the budget will be too small for the group ^'s needs.

12. She ^2B^'ll have to make all the arrangements on her own. ^1A^

13. "If you say it is important, then we will have to consider it our team ^1A^'s best chance at the championship."

14. The players will be given special passes before the games. *NONE*

15. The heiress ^1A^' inheritance was far more than she had expected.

SOLUTION TO EXERCISE 3A
Chapter 4   *APOSTROPHE*

1. You cannot always tell t^{3A}'s from +^{3A}'s.

2. You have used connective and^{3B}'s too many times in your essay.

3. Be sure that your letter contains enough you^{3B}'s.

4. I am looking for your loafers; where are your size 8^{3A}'s?

5. The CPU^{3C}'s will be turned off for maintenance after midnight. *OR NONE*

6. As the CRT^{3C}'s were turned on, the message let everyone know there would be problems all day. *OR NONE*

7. The champion will earn A^{3A}'s on the evaluations.

8. The older PDR^{3C}'s can be stacked at the end of the lot. *OR NONE*

9. The computer printouts made the difference between 3^{3A}'s and 8^{3A}'s difficult to see.

10. The poker player could not decide whether to keep the 10^{3A}'s or 2^{3A}'s.

SOLUTION TO EXERCISE 3B
Chapter 4　　　APOSTROPHE

1.　As you review these papers, check for missing t *3A,* 's at the end of sentences.

2.　The consumer price index (CPI) is frequently revised, but the CPI *3C,* 's do not change all the other indicators. *OR NONE*

3.　The letters must be completed by the end of today *1A,* 's shift.

4.　You have used too many pauses and uh *3B,* 's in your sales presentation.

5.　Additional firefighters were needed to battle the fire *1A,* 's forward movement.

6.　Three additional CTI *3C,* 's will be needed to complete the assembly of the Model 331. *OR NONE*

7.　Make the title tell a story. Use it to grab a reader *1A,* 's attention.

8.　"Excuse me, can you guide me to the rack with size 34 *3A* 's?"

9.　They *2B,* 'll all fit if we rearrange them according to size instead of color.

10.　Any more ORU *3C,* 's we need will require additional modification. *OR NONE*

11.　I hope his conscience doesn *2B,* 't bother him tomorrow.

12.　We cannot accept any more trade-ins of last year *1A,* 's model.

13.　Patents will be issued for all of the inventor *1A,* 's inventions even though he will not be selling them to a manufacturer.

14.　James *1A,* ' leadership makes the group work together well as a team.

15.　The patience of all of the employees will be needed for the new plan to work. *NONE*

SOLUTION TO EXERCISE 1
Chapter 5   *QUOTATION MARKS*

1. We will probably sing 1C "Auld Lang Syne 1C" again this New Year's Eve.

2. After she published her book, Emma appeared on 1D "The Bill Morgan Show 1D" to answer questions.

3. The assignment covered the last chapter, 1A "Causes of the War. 1A"

4. The authors needed more information for their article on baseball— 1B "Greats of the 50's. 1B"

5. Of all his hits the one I liked best was 1C "Baby, I Love You. 1C"

6. The morning program on WBGA is 1D "Wake Up With Wanda. 1D"

7. His recent publications included two articles, 1B "New Issues in Economic Policy 1B" and 1B "Global Economic Change Creates Opportunity." 1B

8. When she finishes the editing, her new book, *Help for the Hassled*, will be ready for publication. NONE

9. The radio announcer began the series with two new songs, 1C "He's in Love 1C" and 1C "Summer Beat." 1C

10. The most quoted chapter in Dr. Martinez' new book is 1A "Chapter 4, Finding Your Place. 1A"

SOLUTION TO EXERCISE 2A
Chapter 5   *QUOTATION MARKS*

1. I have heard him pronounce the word ^{2D}"caterlog.^{2D}"

2. The word ^{2D}"read^{2D}" can be present tense or past tense depending on its context.

3. The boxes were labeled both ^{2D}"flammable^{2D}" and ^{2D}"inflammable^{2D}"; no wonder it confused people.

4. The computer programmer answered that the problem was caused by an ^{2C}"unresolved circular memory access$_{2C}$" within the program.

5. Check closely to see that all the homonyms like ^{2D}"sale^{2D}" and ^{2D}"sail^{2D}" are correctly used in your writing.

6. Fortunately the clerk had marked the receipt ^{2B}"paid^{2B}" so there was no question about the payment.

7. Even though Mark did not know what she meant, the technician explained that the problem was an ^{2C}"extended condenser reaction^{2C}" to the weather.

8. Dr. Martinez had initialed the chart ^{2B}"DVM,^{2B}"^{2C} and the new nurse misunderstood.

9. We should not answer all the questions with other questions. *NONE*

10. Brenda could not think of a reply except that she really didn't ^{2A}"wanna^{2A}" help with the decorating.

SOLUTION TO EXERCISE 2B
Chapter 5   *QUOTATION MARKS*

1. We will be able to sing both **1C**"Auld Lang Syne**1C**"and **1C**"Holiday Cheer**1C**"in the concert.

2. As you write the response letters, be sure not to use any long words like **2D**"anticipatory**2D**" or **2D**"cogitations**2D**"; use simpler words like **2D**"planning**2D**"and **2D**"thoughts.**2D**"

3. Helena Plumb blasted the planning commission for a new sports franchise in her column, **1B**"No Hope for the Impossible,**1B**"which was in yesterday's paper.

4. You will see a major contrast between Ted's character in an early chapter like **1A**"Chapter 2, Which Way?**1A**"and the later chapters like **1A**"Chapter 17, Division of Labor.**1A**"

5. Linguists, those who study languages scientifically, follow the patterns of words common in several languages like the words for **2D**"mother,**2D**""father,**2D**"or **2D**"uncle.**2D**"

6. The doctor told the family that **2C**"vertebral osteoporosis**2C**"caused their grandmother's pain.

7. When she joined station WGGM, Wilma Buckman became the producer of **1D**"Late Night Life.**1D**"

8. Dear Mrs. Smiley:

    We cannot accept your article, **1B**"Tough Times on Wall Street,**1B**" at this time because our next issues are already planned. We wish you luck submitting it elsewhere.

9. The program manager at the radio station would not allow the announcers to play songs such as **1D**"Friendly Faces**1D**"or **1D**"Old Patterns**1D**"because they did not fit with the new programming approach.

10. Like most authors, you can break the writing of a book into chapters to organize the work. **NONE**

11. They changed the evening news program from **1D**"News Day Review**1D**"to **1D**"City Watch**1D**" because the market researchers said the sample audience liked it better.

12. Josie insisted she **2A**"seen**2A**"the entire incident, but no one believed her.

13. Frank Smaller wrote both the words and music to his hit **1C**"Run Far—Run Fast.**1C**"

14. The secretary labeled the envelope **2B**"first class**2B**"so there would be no doubt about its status.

15. The February issue of *Spelunkers' Digest* carried an article, **1B**"Big Holes—Little Holes,**1B**" about recent cave discoveries.

SOLUTION TO EXERCISE 3A
Chapter 5   *QUOTATION MARKS*

1. *3A* " I can't understand you, *3A* " Tami replied into the receiver of the phone.

2. *3A* " I won't be able to help you, *3A* " Cindy explained. *3A* "I have to catch my bus. *3A* "

3. Miguel's mother said, *3A* "You shouldn't always answer with just one word like *2C* 'nope *2C* ' or *2C* 'huh. *2C* ' *3A* "

4. Let me cite an example from Tobin's article:

   3C " The issue cannot be settled by the decision on the new law. Although the decision will clear up some outstanding legal questions, it will not be a complete resolution because too many people still misunderstand the reasons why it is necessary.

   3C " In addition, we will not be able to settle the funding issues before the deadline for a smooth project start. For this reason the project will be behind schedule before it begins. *3C* "

5. During the argument Rick countered, *3A* "Your solution is not acceptable to anyone except you. *3A* "

6. As Tracy left the stage you could hear her mutter the lines, *3A* "Don't yell at me; don't even talk to me. *3A* "

7. Akeo's answer in the interview included his mother's exact words, *3A* "She said, *3A* 'You will always be a winner. *3A* ' Now that I really feel like one, I believe her. *3A* "

8. *3A* "Don't eat any more cookie dough, *3A* " Ellie insisted to her brother. *3A* "We need all of it to finish the cookies. *3A* "

9. The President stated that he would propose a new economic policy which would help deal with the financial concerns of many businesses. *NONE*

10. *3A* "We can't fill all of the positions until next week, *3A* " Miss Jarvis explained.

SOLUTION TO EXERCISE 3B
Chapter 5   *QUOTATION MARKS*

1. " *3A* Will you please set the table? " *3A* asked Mrs. Martinez as she prepared the holiday meal.

2. " *3A* I cannot believe, " *3A* Gary insisted, " *3A* that you have changed so little since I saw you last." *3A*

3. Please make sure that your memo does not make any mistakes with "to," *2D* "two," *2D 2D 2D* and "too." *2D 2D*

4. You will find your answer in the next to the last chapter, *1A* "Patterns for Change. *1A* "

5. The band played *1C* "When We Part *1C* " as the last song at the dance.

6. The commission chairperson directed the members, *3A* "Let's begin the session today with a look at 'Chapter 4, Recommended Alternatives.' *1A* " *3A*

7. " *3A* *1A* We cannot afford to ignore the recommendations, *3A* " the chairperson stated. *3A* "The plan must be carried out right away and funding must be provided on a continuing basis." *3A*

8. The judge's remarks on the suit were included in the article.

3C " Nowhere in the testimony did I find just cause for the actions which the defendant took. On the other hand, I cannot say that his actions were not provoked by the circumstances surrounding the case. The statute is not clear on this specific point in question.

3C " My examination of the case law yields no clear direction. For these reasons, the suit will be dropped; however, further action on other grounds will be possible." *3C*

9. The producers were not successful trying to find a buyer for the new series, *1D* "Who's At Home?" *1D*

10. The most useful information was in *Time*, *1B* "A Portrait of a Leader." *1B*

11. McClaren offered a solution to the problem with the *2C* "rotating helix inference pattern, *2C* " but it was too theoretical to be useful.

12. " *3A* I can't wait, *3A* " Theresa muttered as she scooted out of line. *3A* "I have to check in at the boarding gate, or I'll miss my plane." *3A*

13. Pete wrote the lyrics to *1C* "She's Got the Feelin'" *1C* one month before Midori completed the music.

14. When she left the party, Nancy did not show her concern, but later she voiced it to everyone with her sarcastic remarks. *NONE*

15. The latest issue of *Newslook* has a review of the article, *1B* "Foreign Policy: Points to Ponder." *1B*

SOLUTION TO EXERCISE 1
Chapter 6   *HYPHEN*

1. You will not be able to buy state *1C*-of *1C*-the *1C*-art gifts at the department store.

2. With the coming of spring we will not be able to use the motor *1B*-driven raking machine from last year.

3. The double *1A*-check of all the instruments will happen on the night shift.

4. She always approaches projects with a devil *1C*-may *1C*-care attitude.

5. The typical low *1B*-volume, well *1B*-designed cap monitor will not be available until the beginning of fall.

6. Even though he is a high ranking sprinter, his efforts in the 10 *1B*-kilometer race will depend on his long *1B*-distance conditioning.

7. We will be making long *1B*-term commitments to the new teams as soon as their rankings are established. *1B*

8. They teased him about being an "over *1C*-the *1C*-hill *1C*-grump."

9. The photographer switched lenses on the camera and adjusted the lighting to prepare for the close *1A*-ups of the family.

10. The engineers designed the mechanism to be a self *1B*-actuating, solid *1B*-lever device that can be used in a variety of situations.

11. At the end of each chapter you will find a cross *1B*-referenced list of the most important ideas.

12. Nothing can match the thirst *1B*-quenching ability of water fresh from a spring.

13. Be sure that your manuscript has a one *1B*-inch margin on all edges.

14. Even with all of the possibilities, the leaders could not agree on a new rental policy for the group. *NONE*

15. Sylvia won the award as the best all *1B*-around athlete at the track meet.

SOLUTION TO EXERCISE 2A
Chapter 6   *HYPHEN*

1. The new board will be composed of semi **2A** - independent contractors.

2. It will be necessary to re **2A** - create the tax records that were lost in the fire.

3. As you review the report, we hope that you will find that the mater **2B** -
   ials are sufficient.

4. The ambassador's remarks carried a clearly anti **2A** - American tone.

5. In the oldest notebook you will see that she patiently and dili **2B** -
   gently kept records of the trip to the West.

6. The self **2A** - made millionaire will be leading the conference.

7. Our ex **2A** - mayor will not be attending the dedication ceremony this year.

8. The mid **2A** - January date will allow plenty of time for addi **2B** -
   tional planning.

9. The anti **2A** - intellectual mood gradually changed as more people understood the issues
   involved.

10. The clerk re **2A** - marked the ticket in time for the sale to begin.

SOLUTION TO EXERCISE 2B
Chapter 6   *HYPHEN*

1. Does your brother *1C* -in -*1C* law plan to sell his boat and trailer?

2. No one can predict whether the matter *1C* -of -*1C* fact approach she used will please the customer.

3. Do you think the jury will be able to ignore the indisput *2B* - able facts the lawyer outlined in the speech?

4. We will be developing several low *1B* -cost options for the project.

5. The historians will have to re *2A* -create all of the documents from the fragments that survived the fire.

6. I believe that Jose is ready with an up *1C* -to -*1C* date report.

7. If you will include a self *1B* -addressed envelope with your request, you are more likely to get a quick response.

8. When the vice *1A* -consul of the embassy approved the plans, she considered some of them short -term solutions, and she considered others long -term relief.

9. The professor was an expert in post *1B* - *2A* Civil War *1B* history.

10. The engineer described the invention as an air *1B* -cooled, high *1B* -capacity power unit.

11. The high *1B* -priced, old *1B* -fashioned materials will not work for the new design.

12. In the case of the older items on the shelf, the clerks will have to wait until mid *2A* -January to reorganize the stock.

13. The trans *2A* -Alaska pipeline is able to provide a steady supply of crude oil for U.S. motorists.

14. We must not create a recreation site that will harm the endangered species. *NONE*

15. After he was elected secretary *1A* -treasurer of the club, Kuang-Fu realized that he would have most of the work.

SOLUTION TO EXERCISE 3A
Chapter 6   *HYPHEN*

1. You will find that working with twenty ^{3A}-five children in a preschool class is a tremendous challenge.

2. The two ^{3A}-thirds majority needed to pass the bill will not be available until Thursday.

3. When you paint the sign, be sure to spell the word *Eddie's* E -d -d -i -e -'s and not E -d -d -y -'s.

4. Sheila was so shaken by the accident that her conversation was unusual, "I -I -I couldn't stop in t -t -time."

5. You will have to carry both 25 - and 50 -pound bags as you load the truck.

6. The Panthers picked up a 4 -3 win on their way to the championship.

7. Even though you do not pronounce all the letters k -n -o -t is definitely a different word than n -a -u -g -h -t.

8. My graphic presentation will reflect about two -fifths of the complete written version of the report.

9. Helen replied, "I w -w -w -will not accept your apology."

10. At the end of the survey the first -, second -, and third -ranked factors will need further study.

SOLUTION TO EXERCISE 3B
Chapter 6   *HYPHEN*

1.   The club kept one-third of its money in an interest-bearing checking account and the other two-thirds in a short-term certificate of deposit. *(3A, 1B)*

2.   The fans continued to cheer as the teams went into overtime to settle the 2-2 score. *(3A, 1B, 3A)*

3.   He slowed the car as he approached the 35 mile-an-hour speed zone. *(1C 1C)*

4.   The self-proclaimed leader of the group provided a clear focus for their efforts. *(2A or 1B)*

5.   Even though it was once stained, you will have to re-treat the lumber before it can be used on the new deck. *(2A)*

6.   The test was completed at 10-, 30-, and 60-minute intervals. *(3D 3D 3D)*

7.   The need for a pro-African policy was made clear to all of the delegates. *(2A)*

8.   Carlson had no idea that *wrought iron* was spelled *w-r-o-u-g-h-t.* *(3C 3C 3C 3C 3C 3C)*

9.   Jill's brother-in-law met her at the mall to help her shop for her husband's gift. *(1C 1C)*

10.   With his grandfather's help, John was able to develop a pay-as-you-go plan to pay for his new car. *(1C 1C 1C)*

11.   Frank was elected secretary-treasurer of the group because he owned a computer to help handle the lengthy correspond-ence and finances. *(1A, 2B)*

12.   Without a minimum water level following the drought, the reservoir owned by the city could not meet the water needs of the small community. *NONE*

13.   The well-known actor rejected the part because he would be in fewer than one-fifth of the major scenes. *(1B, 3A)*

14.   U-u-ugh! I can't stand the taste of that toothpaste. *(3B 3B)*

15.   As Betsy studied the weather-beaten old building for her photographic session, she saw several artistic possibil-ities for the magazine cover. *(1B, 2B)*

SOLUTION TO EXERCISE 1
Chapter 7   *PARENTHESES*

1. When you file the PRS *1D* (Proposed Reservation System *1D*) form make sure that all the information in Part IV is complete.

2. The administration department has become a catch-all for many organizations *1E* (e.g., accounting, security, printing, and others). *1E*

3. No further action can be taken on the DLR *1D* (direct labor report *1D*) because the increase in budget is not available until after the first of the year.

4. Her words began to annoy the audience *1A* (including many of her former friends and allies) as she made her way from point to point.

5. *1A* How can we develop an interface with the new equipment *1E* (i.e., how can what we have work with the additional machines we plan to buy)?

6. The team's equipment *1A* (including even extra jerseys and practice uniforms *1E*) remains the *1A* property of the league.

7. As the students began the art course, they found they needed supplies *1C* (brushes, pencils, erasers, and paints) to begin the first project. *1C*

8. When you complete your monthly labor report, include all the data from your organization. *1C* (Be certain to include the remaining budget, hours worked, and units shipped.) *1A* *1A*

9. The committee members *1C* (Margaret, Gale, Gary, and Al) will attend the meeting if you *1C* feel their help is needed.

10. I cannot see any way to break the pattern of failure unless we restructure the department *1B* (I know you don't want that). *1B*

SOLUTION TO EXERCISE 2A
Chapter 7   PARENTHESES

1. The minimum value is 27.5 pounds; it has been established by solid experiments *2B* (Wilson, 1987 *)* . *2B*

2. The most reliable information points toward the conclusion that the rates will decline next year. *(* See Figure 7. *) 2A*

3. The main points were made in the conclusion, but other useful information was in the *2A* special matrix and the references *(* see Section 4 *) . 2A*

4. You will find the results detailed in the accompanying tables *2A* *(* see Appendix 1 *2A* *)* . *2A*

5. The data in the study revealed a lower worker absence rate *2B* (Janforth, 1990 *2B* *)* .

6. As you complete the installation of the motor cover *2A* *(* paragraphs 7 through 12 *) 2A* , keep all other parts out of the way to avoid confusion.

7. Your use of the initial meter settings *2A* *(* Table 3 *2A* *)* will help make the test a valid one.

8. The relationships of the various chemicals were established by earlier experiments *2B* (Amstad, 1966 *) 2B* while the complete matrix was described later by Laura Smith *2B* (Smith, 1977 *)* . *2B*

9. In the early stages of your work *2A* *(* Chapters 1-20 *2A* *)* you will need more time; in the later stages *(* Chapters 21-38 *)* you will not.

10. The reliability of the new process has been confirmed *2A* *2A* *(* Hancock, 1988 *2B* *) 2B* , but it is still not widely used.

SOLUTION TO EXERCISE 2B
Chapter 7   *PARENTHESES*

1. The newest experiments *2B* (Westfall, 1990 *2B*) confirm the results of the studies done by Betty Campbell (Campbell, 1987). *2B*

2. William Hewlitt was recently elected president of ICBA *2B* (International Congress of *1D* Business Associates). *1D*

3. With few exceptions the pattern repeats regardless of temperature changes. *2A* (See Figure 6. *2A*)

4. The IDU *1D* (International Detailers Union *1D*) provides scholarships for several college students.

5. While the negotiations continue, you will have to keep most points confidential *1E* (i.e., you cannot issue press releases and you cannot make stock trades). *1E*

6. The champions of the NFC *1D* (National Football Conference *1D*) and AFC *1D* (American Football Conference) meet every year in the Superbowl in January.

7. The new model will include several new features, but the most notable is a TAB *1D* (total access bracket). *1D*

8. The students on the committee have completed the project *1B* (I never doubted that they would) in record time.

9. Many newer cars have an ABS *1B* *1D* (antilock braking system *1D*) as standard equipment; others have it as an option.

10. Additional research following Answell's discovery *2B* (Patten, 1987 *2B*) confirmed the results and lead to a more useful product.

11. Hundreds of antiques *1C* (furniture, tools, lanterns, pictures, and kitchen utensils *1C*) were auctioned when the old barn was torn down.

12. The job application process and hiring procedure at most companies are governed by regulations from the EEOC *1D* (Equal Employment Opportunity Commission). *1D*

13. As you wax the car, be sure to polish the wheel lug nuts too. *1D* *NONE*

14. If you believe Okano's idea *2B* (Okano, 1988 *2B*), then you will also have to agree with Winston's refinements (Winston, 1990). *2B*

15. You will find the corresponding data in detail later in the chapter. *2B* *2A* (See Table II. *2A*)

SOLUTION TO EXERCISE 3A
Chapter 7   *PARENTHESES*

1. The team will need several new tactics for the new season: *3A* (1) *3A* it will have to develop a stronger defense, *3A* (2) *3A* it will have to develop better scouting reports, and (3) it will need a motivational leader. *3A   3A*

2. The lease reads, "The Lessee/User shall pay to Acme, Inc. the base rent of twelve thousand dollars *(*$12,000*)* in three *(3)* installments."

3. We have prevented further damage by taking the following preventive actions: *3B 3B 3B 3B* (1) *3A* (1) *3A* buying reinforced window frames, *(2)* installing new latches, and *(3)* replacing older hinges. *3A   3A*   *3A   3A*

4. We need to go further because we cannot find the following information: *3A* (1) *3A* last year's figures, *3A* (2) *3A* enough information on our competitors and *(3)* the research on the new product. *3A   3A*

5. The official report read, "The crash occurred on lap thirty-three *3B* (33) *3B* of the race."

6. As the figures were compiled, the winners were decided because they had more than seventeen correct responses. *NONE*

7. The folklore about the mansion said that it was *3A* (1) *3A* haunted by the first owner, *3A* (2) *3A* sold every two years because of water problems, and *(3)* almost destroyed because it was not properly constructed. *3A   3A*

8. Most nutritionists still agree that balance in your diet is achieved by *3A* (a) *3A* a variety of foods, *3A* (b) *3A* moderation in that not all foods are from the same groups, and *(c)* skillful selection and cooking. *3A   3A*

9. Please clarify your order. Do you want four *3B* (4) *3B* dozen or forty *3B* (40) *3B* dozen of the Model 41B?

10. You will be able to pass the certification exam by *3A* (1) *3A* studying all of the material, *3A* (2) *3A* committing the study guide to memory, and *(3)* getting a good night's sleep the night before. *3A   3A*

SOLUTION TO EXERCISE 3B
Chapter 7   *PARENTHESES*

1. The juniors on the team **1C** (Susan, Katrina, Natalie, and Patty **1C**) will be returning for another season next year.

2. Miss Sanchez' order called for two hundred **3B** (200 **3B**) of the 16-valve units.

3. Spectators will be allowed to use the reserved seating later in the game. **1B** (After all the hassle no one will want to sit there anyway.) **1B**

4. The sale of the company was approved by the SEC **1D** (Securities Exchange Commission **1D**) because all of the requirements were met at the time of the sale.

5. As the planning commission considers the application, several factors must be studied: **3A** (1) **3A** the effect of changes on jobs, **3A** (2) **3A** the need for additional water facilities, and (3) the time frame for completing the project.

6. Carol Simpson will lead the new committee **3A** (I hope she does not meet opposition **3A** **1B**) **1B** and complete the development effort.

7. The study which lead to the recommendation **2B** (Barnes, 1988 **2B**) clarified all of the issues.

8. The compiled data **2A** (see p. 52 **2A**) clearly establishes the need for an additional hospital in the area.

9. The engineers calculated the LCC **1D** (Life Cycle Cost **1D**) for the fleet of new airplanes.

10. Using extreme caution and patience **1E** (i.e., not starting too early **1E**) will allow you to solve many of the problems without additional testing.

11. No additional funds will be available from the Historical Foundation Fund for the rebuilding of the old building. *NONE*

12. In addition to the preliminary results **2A** (see Chapter 3 **2A**), the complete data taken during the test show a clear improvement in the water quality. (See Appendix B.) **2A**

13. All of the equipment for the team **1A** (including all playing gear and uniforms **2A**) was delayed at the airport causing a rush to prepare for the game. **1A**

14. The FCC **1D** (Federal Communications Commission **1D**) will need to approve the new licenses for the transmitter, but the operation will still be on schedule.

15. Preparations for the project will include the following: **3A** (1) **3A** funding, **3A** (2) **3A** approvals, and (3) detailed site plans. **3A** **3A**

SOLUTION TO EXERCISE 1
Chapter 8   *END MARKS*

1. Please make sure that your forms are complete. *1A*

2. The supplies account in next year's budget will need only a slight increase of 2. 1 *1D* percent. *1A*

3. Be sure to make the following preparations for the test:
   1C 1. Study the material thoroughly
   1C 2. Rest well the night before
   1C 3. Bring sharp pencils

4. Important factors. *1E* Historians have discussed the causes of the Civil War in the United States for many years. *1A* Although they mention many factors, most agree on the economic forces that separated the North and South. *1A*

5. Mr. *1F* and Mrs. *1F* Williams will participate in the panel discussion. *1A*

6. He left his new address: 4144 E. *1F* Jefferson Rd., Huntsville, VA 12211. *1F* *1A*

7. Sylvia, please arrange for the transportation to the convention. *1A*

8. James T. *1F* Wilson completed the final statistics of the study using a computer program from the university. *1A*

9. I have not agreed with the recommendation for the following reasons:
   1C a. No funds
   1C b. No time
   1C c. No available people

10. You will find that the captain has all of the necessary information. *1A*

11. The test will use the oldest of the patterns. *1A*

12. Even though cases of the new adhesive will weigh over 300 lbs., *1F* we can ship them overnight. *1A*

13. We can still make a profit with costs that are 113 percent higher, but the prices will have to be stable. *1A*

14. My greatest fear is that we will run out of time before we can get the project finished. *1A*

15. Alan Lumowski, *1F* M. D. *1F* , will be the speaker at the monthly meeting. *1A*

SOLUTION TO EXERCISE 2A
Chapter 8   *END MARKS*

1. What is the latest date that I can reserve a room and plane ticket? *2A*

2. How will the new department be organized? *2A*

3. Is this the only size seven dress in this beautiful blue? *2A*

4. "You can't tell which one is older, can you? *2A*" Theresa asked as she examined the antiques.

5. Will you be traveling during the holiday break? *2A*

6. Most authorities agree that the original idea was developed in 1966 (?). *2B*

7. William will be installed as president of the club next month, won't he? *2A*

8. Will Carl Hopkins, the manager of the store, interview the new applicants? *2A*

9. Did Millie really tell you, "No more carts were available"? *2A*

10. He was born early this century; April 26 (?), 1914. *2B*

SOLUTION TO EXERCISE 2B
Chapter 8   *END MARKS*

1. Will you be attending the meeting Friday afternoon ? *2A*

2. The president of the club has the responsibility for conducting the meeting . *1A*

3. Bring me that adjustable wrench. *1A*

4. The price of the new radio will be $29 *1D* .99 . *1A*

5. When you have finished with the painting, complete these jobs:
   1C a. Remove the trash in the garage
   1C b. Sweep the garage
   1C c. Mop the garage floor

6. How many pages have you read in that new book ? *2A*

7. The team finished the season with a winning record, but the coach was not satisfied . *1A*

8. His mother inquired, "Will you help me with the dishes ?" *2A*

9. <u>Literature study</u> . *1E* Many courses in American literature are organized around the major historical periods. *1A* These courses are also organized around other topics such as authors or literature types. *1A* In all cases the courses involve investigating the major authors and movements. *1A*

10. The discovery of the artifacts at the ruins shift the date of occupancy to 1150 (?) . *2B* *1A*

11. Joseph, do not turn on the other machine . *1A*

12. "How will we find all of the books if we do not catalog them ?" *2A* the bookstore owner asked the new employee. *1A*

13. If you drive along Miles Ave . *1F* until you cross the bridge, you will see all the major sites . *1A*

14. The soccer game ended with a score of 1 to 0 after playing two overtime periods . *1A*

15. After Alicia passed the exam, she opened her office as a C. *1F* P. *1F* A. *1F* and began her practice . *1A*

SOLUTION TO EXERCISE 3A
Chapter 8   *END MARKS*

1. That was a great game! *3A*

2. You were great! *3A* Thanks so much.

3. Gosh! *3B* Can anything else happen?

4. What is the point of your objection? *NONE*

5. Help! *3B* I'm dropping all these packages.

6. Attention! *3B* Your commander has just entered.

7. Go to your room now! *3A*

8. I know you don't believe me, but he is the man I saw! *3A*

9. Hurray! *3B* We finished the project.

10. Emi replied quickly, "You can't mean it! *3A* "

Note: Use of exclamation marks may vary.

SOLUTION TO EXERCISE 3B
Chapter 8   *END MARKS*

1. How right you are ! ^{3A}

2. "We cannot have all of the workers on first shift ! " Pat, the manager, exclaimed. ^{3A}

3. We cannot believe that every task is complete, can we ? ^{2A}

4. We will need the resources of the executive committee, won't we ? ^{2A}

5. Is this the last of the forms we need to process ? ^{2A}

6. Of the 320 (?) applications how many are from Texas ? ^{2B} ^{2A}

7. We will need all of the following items for the proposal:
   ^{1C} 1. Cost estimates
   ^{1C} 2. A clear schedule
   ^{1C} 3. An explanation of the plan

8. Mr . Smiley, will you help with the treasurer's report ? ^{1F} ^{2A}

9. Whew ! That car came really close. ^{3B}

10. We cannot win if many of our players have injuries. *NONE*

11. City plans . The leaders of the community will plan and develop a new park system. With the help of many clubs and organizations the new parks will be ready by next summer. Cooperation will make it possible. ^{1E}

12. There you are, Ms . Arnberry. Will there be anything else ? ^{1F} ^{2A}

13. Just saying that the price is between $200 and $300 is not enough. Be specific and say the price is $234.99. ^{1A}

14. The new paving project will begin on Madison Ave . next week. ^{1D} ^{1F}

15. Stop ! Don't touch the hot iron. ^{3B}

Note: Use of exclamation marks may vary.

COMPACT APOSTROPHE SUMMARY

1. Use apostrophes to indicate POSSESSION.
   A. Singular words
   B. Plural words

POSSESSION

"Plus" Diagram

	Singular	Plural
Regular	boy	boys
Possessive	boy's	boys'

2. Use apostrophes to indicate DELETION (contraction forms).
   A. Numbers
   B. Letters

   C. In dialogue to show pronunciation
   D. Certain invented expressions

DELETION

A. '76   (1976)
B. can't   (cannot)
   doesn't (does not)
   nat'l   (national)
C. "Well, if you are goin', then I am too."
D. The supervisor ok'd the order.

3. Use apostrophes to indicate PLURALS of symbols and abbreviations.
   A. Characters (letters, numbers, or symbols)

   B. Words referred to as words
   C. Abbreviations
      (without is also accepted when abbreviation is all capital letters)

PLURALS

A. a's   3's
   t's   &'s   i's
   I am looking for your size 5's.
B. In your speech you used too many *and's.*
C. CPU's   (CPUs)
   MPI's   (MPIs)

COMPACT COLON SUMMARY

1. Use colons for Mechanical SEPARATION (SHORT items).
   A. Hours and minutes
   B. Biblical chapter and verse
   C. Title and subtitle

   D. Proportions (ratios)

SEPARATION (SHORT)
   A. 9:45 p.m.   6:30 a.m.
   B. James 2:4   Exodus 12:1–10
   C. *Punctuation: An Introduction*
      Columbus: A Man of His Times
   D. 3:2   13:1

2. Use colons for Mechanical SEPARATION (LONG items).
   A. Salutation and text of a speech

   B. Resolution and following statement
   C. Speaker and lines in a play or script

   D. Publishing mechanics
      • Journal citation from volume (short form)
        Separates volume number from page
      • Place and publisher

      • Separate acts and scenes of plays

SEPARATION (LONG)
   A. Mr. Chairman, Miss Spencer, members of the club: thank you for inviting me to speak this evening.
   B. Resolved: The legislature should plan for new schools.
   C. Bob: I can't believe you.
      Sam: You don't have a choice.
   D.
      • Williams, Julie. "Recovering from Loss," *Helping Hand*, 62:57–59, September 1989.
      • Carbunkle, Amanda. *Hail to the Chef.* New York: Gourmet Publishing Company, 1988.
      • *Romeo and Juliet* III:ii

3. Use colons in CORRESPONDENCE mechanics.
   A. Author and typist's initials
   B. Salutation from business letter
   C. Carbon copy or photocopy notation

   D. Memo headings and information

   E. Subject line in letter

CORRESPONDENCE
   A. KJE:jb (letters and memos)
   B. Dear Ms. Slater:
   C. cc: William Gold
      pc: Maria Reeves
   D.   To: Jim Simpson
         From: Kim Lee Chin
         Date: June 14, 19--
         Subject: Budget Projections
   E. Subject: Your Request for Information

4. Use colons to INTRODUCE additional content.
   A. List
      • Displayed

      • Internal in sentence
        (Do not separate objects from prepositions or verbs.)
   B. Extended quotation
      • Displayed

      • Internal

   C. Extended explanation

   D. Amplification for emphasis
   E. Additional detail

   F. Connected ideas
      • Additional information
      • Transitional expressions (e.g., i.e., for example, that is)

      • Repeated structure

INTRODUCE
   A.
      • Bring the following items:
        - Chips
        - Pretzels
        - Crackers
      • You may bring the following supplies to the test: pencils, an eraser, and a ruler.
   B.
      • Although he was not a gardener, Mark Twain noted certain distinctions:
        I know the taste of the watermelon which has been honestly come by and I know the taste of the watermelon which has been acquired by art. Both taste good, but the experienced know which tastes best.
      • Mark Twain showed his cynic's disdain for telling the truth when he said: "Lying is universal—we *all* do it; we all *must* do it. Therefore, the wise thing is for us to diligently train ourselves to lie thoughtfully. . ."
   C. Please let me explain this way: the whole is sometimes greater than the sum of its parts.
   D. He cared only about one possession: his car.
   E. For Sale: mountain cabin
      Note: The test results must be recorded at this time.
   F.
      • He toiled all his life: such was his plight.
      • Do not use periods with abbreviations for agencies: e.g., FBI, CIA, or DOD.
        Security guards will provide protection: that is, they will be guarding the door and escorting people to their cars.
      • She can be elected: she must be elected.

COMPACT COLON SUMMARY

1. Use colons for Mechanical SEPARATION (SHORT items).
   A. Hours and minutes
   B. Biblical chapter and verse
   C. Title and subtitle

   D. Proportions (ratios)

SEPARATION (SHORT)
A. 9:45 p.m.   6:30 a.m.
B. James 2:4   Exodus 12:1–10
C. *Punctuation: An Introduction*
   Columbus: A Man of His Times
D. 3:2   13:1

---

2. Use colons for Mechanical SEPARATION (LONG items).
   A. Salutation and text of a speech

   B. Resolution and following statement
   C. Speaker and lines in a play or script

   D. Publishing mechanics
      • Journal citation from volume (short form)
        Separates volume number from page
      • Place and publisher

      • Separate acts and scenes of plays

SEPARATION (LONG)
A. Mr. Chairman, Miss Spencer, members of the club: thank you for inviting me to speak this evening.
B. Resolved: The legislature should plan for new schools.
C. Bob: I can't believe you.
   Sam: You don't have a choice.
D.
   • Williams, Julie. "Recovering from Loss," *Helping Hand*, 62:57–59, September 1989.
   • Carbunkle, Amanda. *Hail to the Chef.* New York: Gourmet Publishing Company, 1988.
   • *Romeo and Juliet* III:ii

---

3. Use colons in CORRESPONDENCE mechanics.
   A. Author and typist's initials
   B. Salutation from business letter
   C. Carbon copy or photocopy notation

   D. Memo headings and information

   E. Subject line in letter

CORRESPONDENCE
A. KJE:jb (letters and memos)
B. Dear Ms. Slater:
C. cc: William Gold
   pc: Maria Reeves
D.   To: Jim Simpson
      From: Kim Lee Chin
      Date: June 14, 19--
      Subject: Budget Projections
E. Subject: Your Request for Information

---

4. Use colons to INTRODUCE additional content.
   A. List
      • Displayed

      • Internal in sentence
        (Do not separate objects from prepositions or verbs.)
   B. Extended quotation
      • Displayed

      • Internal

   C. Extended explanation

   D. Amplification for emphasis
   E. Additional detail

   F. Connected ideas
      • Additional information
      • Transitional expressions (e.g., i.e., for example, that is)

      • Repeated structure

INTRODUCE
A.
   • Bring the following items:
      - Chips
      - Pretzels
      - Crackers
   • You may bring the following supplies to the test: pencils, an eraser, and a ruler.
B.
   • Although he was not a gardener, Mark Twain noted certain distinctions:
      I know the taste of the watermelon which has been honestly come by and I know the taste of the watermelon which has been acquired by art. Both taste good, but the experienced know which tastes best.
   • Mark Twain showed his cynic's disdain for telling the truth when he said: "Lying is universal—we *all* do it; we all *must* do it. Therefore, the wise thing is for us to diligently train ourselves to lie thoughtfully. . ."
C. Please let me explain this way: the whole is sometimes greater than the sum of its parts.
D. He cared only about one possession: his car.
E. For Sale: mountain cabin
   Note: The test results must be recorded at this time.
F.
   • He toiled all his life: such was his plight.
   • Do not use periods with abbreviations for agencies: e.g., FBI, CIA, or DOD.
     Security guards will provide protection: that is, they will be guarding the door and escorting people to their cars.
   • She can be elected: she must be elected.

COMPACT APOSTROPHE SUMMARY

1. Use apostrophes to indicate POSSESSION.
   A. Singular words
   B. Plural words

POSSESSION

"Plus" Diagram

	Singular	**Plural**
Regular	boy	boys
Possessive	boy's	boys'

2. Use apostrophes to indicate DELETION (contraction forms).
   A. Numbers
   B. Letters

   C. In dialogue to show pronunciation
   D. Certain invented expressions

DELETION

A. '76   (1976)
B. can't   (cannot)
   doesn't (does not)
   nat'l   (national)
C. "Well, if you are goin', then I am too."
D. The supervisor ok'd the order.

3. Use apostrophes to indicate PLURALS of symbols and abbreviations.
   A. Characters (letters, numbers, or symbols)

   B. Words referred to as words
   C. Abbreviations
   (without is also accepted when abbreviation is all capital letters)

PLURALS

A. a's   3's
   t's   &'s   i's
   I am looking for your size 5's.
B. In your speech you used too many *and's.*
C. CPU's   (CPUs)
   MPI's   (MPIs)

COMPACT COLON SUMMARY

1. **Use colons for Mechanical SEPARATION (SHORT items).**
   A. Hours and minutes
   B. Biblical chapter and verse
   C. Title and subtitle

   D. Proportions (ratios)

SEPARATION (SHORT)
A. 9:45 p.m.   6:30 a.m.
B. James 2:4   Exodus 12:1–10
C. *Punctuation: An Introduction*
   Columbus: A Man of His Times
D. 3:2   13:1

---

2. **Use colons for Mechanical SEPARATION (LONG items).**
   A. Salutation and text of a speech

   B. Resolution and following statement
   C. Speaker and lines in a play or script

   D. Publishing mechanics
   • Journal citation from volume (short form)
     Separates volume number from page
   • Place and publisher

   • Separate acts and scenes of plays

SEPARATION (LONG)
A. Mr. Chairman, Miss Spencer, members of the club: thank you for inviting me to speak this evening.
B. Resolved: The legislature should plan for new schools.
C. Bob: I can't believe you.
   Sam: You don't have a choice.
D.
   • Williams, Julie. "Recovering from Loss," *Helping Hand*, 62:57–59, September 1989.
   • Carbunkle, Amanda. *Hail to the Chef.* New York: Gourmet Publishing Company, 1988.
   • *Romeo and Juliet* III:ii

---

3. **Use colons in CORRESPONDENCE mechanics.**
   A. Author and typist's initials
   B. Salutation from business letter
   C. Carbon copy or photocopy notation

   D. Memo headings and information

   E. Subject line in letter

CORRESPONDENCE
A. KJE:jb (letters and memos)
B. Dear Ms. Slater:
C. cc: William Gold
   pc: Maria Reeves
D.   To: Jim Simpson
       From: Kim Lee Chin
       Date: June 14, 19--
   Subject: Budget Projections
E. Subject: Your Request for Information

---

4. **Use colons to INTRODUCE additional content.**
   A. List
   • Displayed

   • Internal in sentence
     (Do not separate objects from prepositions or verbs.)
   B. Extended quotation
   • Displayed

   • Internal

   C. Extended explanation

   D. Amplification for emphasis
   E. Additional detail

   F. Connected ideas
   • Additional information
   • Transitional expressions (e.g., i.e., for example, that is)

   • Repeated structure

INTRODUCE
A.
   • Bring the following items:
       - Chips
       - Pretzels
       - Crackers
   • You may bring the following supplies to the test: pencils, an eraser, and a ruler.
B.
   • Although he was not a gardener, Mark Twain noted certain distinctions:
       I know the taste of the watermelon which has been honestly come by and I know the taste of the watermelon which has been acquired by art. Both taste good, but the experienced know which tastes best.
   • Mark Twain showed his cynic's disdain for telling the truth when he said: "Lying is universal—we *all* do it; we all *must* do it. Therefore, the wise thing is for us to diligently train ourselves to lie thoughtfully. . ."
C. Please let me explain this way: the whole is sometimes greater than the sum of its parts.
D. He cared only about one possession: his car.
E. For Sale: mountain cabin
   Note: The test results must be recorded at this time.
F.
   • He toiled all his life: such was his plight.
   • Do not use periods with abbreviations for agencies: e.g., FBI, CIA, or DOD.
     Security guards will provide protection: that is, they will be guarding the door and escorting people to their cars.
   • She can be elected: she must be elected.

COMPACT COLON SUMMARY

1. Use colons for Mechanical SEPARATION (SHORT items).
   A. Hours and minutes
   B. Biblical chapter and verse
   C. Title and subtitle

   D. Proportions (ratios)

SEPARATION (SHORT)
A. 9:45 p.m.   6:30 a.m.
B. James 2:4   Exodus 12:1–10
C. *Punctuation: An Introduction*
   Columbus: A Man of His Times
D. 3:2   13:1

2. Use colons for Mechanical SEPARATION (LONG items).
   A. Salutation and text of a speech

   B. Resolution and following statement
   C. Speaker and lines in a play or script

   D. Publishing mechanics
   - Journal citation from volume (short form)
     Separates volume number from page
   - Place and publisher

   - Separate acts and scenes of plays

SEPARATION (LONG)
A. Mr. Chairman, Miss Spencer, members of the club: thank you for inviting me to speak this evening.
B. Resolved: The legislature should plan for new schools.
C. Bob: I can't believe you.
   Sam: You don't have a choice.
D.
   - Williams, Julie. "Recovering from Loss," *Helping Hand*, 62:57–59, September 1989.
   - Carbunkle, Amanda. *Hail to the Chef*. New York: Gourmet Publishing Company, 1988.
   - *Romeo and Juliet* III:ii

3. Use colons in CORRESPONDENCE mechanics.
   A. Author and typist's initials
   B. Salutation from business letter
   C. Carbon copy or photocopy notation

   D. Memo headings and information

   E. Subject line in letter

CORRESPONDENCE
A. KJE:jb (letters and memos)
B. Dear Ms. Slater:
C. cc: William Gold
   pc: Maria Reeves
D.   To: Jim Simpson
   From: Kim Lee Chin
   Date: June 14, 19--
   Subject: Budget Projections
E. Subject: Your Request for Information

4. Use colons to INTRODUCE additional content.
   A. List
   - Displayed

   - Internal in sentence
     (Do not separate objects from prepositions or verbs.)
   B. Extended quotation
   - Displayed

   - Internal

   C. Extended explanation

   D. Amplification for emphasis
   E. Additional detail

   F. Connected ideas
   - Additional information
   - Transitional expressions (e.g., i.e., for example, that is)

   - Repeated structure

INTRODUCE
A.
   - Bring the following items:
     - Chips
     - Pretzels
     - Crackers
   - You may bring the following supplies to the test: pencils, an eraser, and a ruler.
B.
   - Although he was not a gardener, Mark Twain noted certain distinctions:
     I know the taste of the watermelon which has been honestly come by and I know the taste of the watermelon which has been acquired by art. Both taste good, but the experienced know which tastes best.
   - Mark Twain showed his cynic's disdain for telling the truth when he said: "Lying is universal—we *all* do it; we all *must* do it. Therefore, the wise thing is for us to diligently train ourselves to lie thoughtfully. . ."
C. Please let me explain this way: the whole is sometimes greater than the sum of its parts.
D. He cared only about one possession: his car.
E. For Sale: mountain cabin
   Note: The test results must be recorded at this time.
F.
   - He toiled all his life: such was his plight.
   - Do not use periods with abbreviations for agencies: e.g., FBI, CIA, or DOD.
     Security guards will provide protection: that is, they will be guarding the door and escorting people to their cars.
   - She can be elected: she must be elected.

COMPACT PARENTHESES SUMMARY

1. Use parentheses to set off INTERRUPTIONS.
   A. Explanations (words, phrases, or clauses)

   B. Comments
   C. Examples

   D. Abbreviations

   E. Transitional expressions (i.e., e.g., that is, for example)

INTERRUPTIONS

A. As you study the report, note the results (including statistics).
   As you study the report (including all supporting material and statistics), note the results.
   As you study the report, note the results. (Be sure to study the tables.)
B. You will find him working (oddly enough) in the garage.
C. Several of the senior players (Ellen, Jackie, Susan) will continue until the end of the season.
D. The CRT (cathode ray tube) has had an important impact on several technological changes.
E. Several artifacts (e.g., a pot, a hammer, a digging tool) were found at the new site.
   The altered committee (i.e., the new officers and members) will develop the new plan.

2. Use parentheses for MECHANICAL POINTING.
   A. References

   B. Citations

MECHANICAL POINTING

A. The performance is outstanding (see Figure 1).
   Profits were higher this quarter. (See Table 7.)
B. As you can conclude from her study (Smith, 1987), the research seems complete.

3. Use parentheses to list or repeat NUMBERS.
   A. List within a sentence
      (letters as an alternate)

   B. Repetition for accuracy

NUMBERS

A. The class president made plans for all the spring activities: (1) the carnival, (2) the final dance, and (3) the special talent show.
   The class president made plans for all the spring activities: (a) the carnival, (b) the final dance, and (c) the special talent show.
B. Please provide sixty (60) dozen of the new washers.

COMPACT PARENTHESES SUMMARY

1. Use parentheses to set off INTERRUPTIONS.
   A. Explanations (words, phrases, or clauses)

   B. Comments
   C. Examples

   D. Abbreviations

   E. Transitional expressions (i.e., e.g., that is, for example)

INTERRUPTIONS
   A. As you study the report, note the results (including statistics).
      As you study the report (including all supporting material and statistics), note the results.
      As you study the report, note the results. (Be sure to study the tables.)
   B. You will find him working (oddly enough) in the garage.
   C. Several of the senior players (Ellen, Jackie, Susan) will continue until the end of the season.
   D. The CRT (cathode ray tube) has had an important impact on several technological changes.
   E. Several artifacts (e.g., a pot, a hammer, a digging tool) were found at the new site.
      The altered committee (i.e., the new officers and members) will develop the new plan.

2. Use parentheses for MECHANICAL POINTING.
   A. References

   B. Citations

MECHANICAL POINTING
   A. The performance is outstanding (see Figure 1).
      Profits were higher this quarter. (See Table 7.)
   B. As you can conclude from her study (Smith, 1987), the research seems complete.

3. Use parentheses to list or repeat NUMBERS.
   A. List within a sentence
      (letters as an alternate)

   B. Repetition for accuracy

NUMBERS
   A. The class president made plans for all the spring activities: (1) the carnival, (2) the final dance, and (3) the special talent show.
      The class president made plans for all the spring activities: (a) the carnival, (b) the final dance, and (c) the special talent show.
   B. Please provide sixty (60) dozen of the new washers.

COMPACT HYPHEN SUMMARY

1. Use hyphens in COMBINED word forms.
   A. Compound nouns

   B. Compound adjectives

   C. Combined phrases

COMBINED
   A. make-believe
      money-maker
      close-up
   B. high-pressure hose
      government-owned equipment
      short-term loan
      10-yard gain
   C. Hole-in-the-wall gang
      stick-in-the-mud
      never-say-die
      mother-in-law

---

2. Use hyphens in INTERNAL word forms.
   A. Some prefixes

   B. Word separations (end of a line)

   (Note: Consult a current dictionary when using hyphens
   with prefixes or for word divisions.)

INTERNAL
   A. (misreading)   re-create
      (capital letter)   anti-British
      (*ex-* and *self-*) ex-president
      (double vowel)   semi-independent
   B. The legislature will not appro-
      priate the funds.

---

3. Use hyphens for MECHANICS.
   A. Numbers

   B. Unusual or extended pronunciations

   C. Letters as letters

   D. Suspended forms

MECHANICS
   A. twenty-three
      two-fifths
      A 4-2 victory really pleased the coach.
      pages 234-238
   B. G-g-glad you could make it.
      Say a-a-h.
   C. The spelling champ spelled *receive* r-e-c-e-i-v-e to win
      the round.
   D. She taught a group of six- and seven-year-olds.
      Lumber may be purchased in 8-, 12-, and 16-foot lengths.

COMPACT QUOTATION MARK SUMMARY

1. Use quotation marks to show TITLES for some artistic works (others use italics/underline).

   A. Chapter

   B. Article

   C. Song
   D. Radio and TV programs

TITLES

   A. After reading the introduction, you should read "Chapter 3: The Golden Basket."
   B. The lead article for the evening edition was "Governors Decide Funding."
   C. Jason B's latest hit is "My Love, You're Special."
   D. Will you watch "Sports Headlines" tonight?

2. Use quotation marks to show a WORD used in a special sense.

   A. Intentional misspelling or poor use of grammar
   B. Used with special expression such as *signed, labeled,* or *marked*
   C. Technical or slang terms

   D. Refer to the word itself
      (Underline or italics is preferred, but quotation marks are also used.)

WORD

   A. I know you don't "wanna."
   B. The letter was signed "Martin Cuzos."

   C. The "rotary sleeve" clutch was used on the new model. No matter how we ask Bill, he "ain't workin' with ya."
   D. Delete "often" in the second sentence.

3. Use quotation marks to show the DIRECT WORDS of a speaker.

   A. Within a sentence

   B. Within another quotation
   C. Long quotations
      • Within text

      • Blocked off (acceptable but not preferred)

DIRECT WORDS

   A. Bill said, "I want to finish the report."
      "This meeting will now come to order," the director announced.
      "Marie," her friend said, "you must finish this project."
   B. Tom said, "Joe's comment was simply, 'Ugh.'"
   C.
      • The speaker closed with these remarks: "The future of this organization is in your hands. We can grow and prosper or languish. The choice is yours." The speaker received a standing ovation.
      • Phyllis showed her feelings when she replied this way:

         "We will not care about the new report until it is complete. Yet you may express my concern to all of the other staff members. No excuses will be allowed."

Usage Notes:
• Place periods and commas inside the quotation marks.
• Place semicolons and colons outside the quotation marks.
• Place dashes and question marks inside or outside the quotation marks depending on whether the sense applies to all or part.
• Long quotations indented from both right and left margins receive no quotation marks.

COMPACT QUOTATION MARK SUMMARY

1. Use quotation marks to show TITLES for some artistic works (others use italics/underline).
   A. Chapter

   B. Article

   C. Song
   D. Radio and TV programs

TITLES

   A. After reading the introduction, you should read "Chapter 3: The Golden Basket."
   B. The lead article for the evening edition was "Governors Decide Funding."
   C. Jason B's latest hit is "My Love, You're Special."
   D. Will you watch "Sports Headlines" tonight?

2. Use quotation marks to show a WORD used in a special sense.
   A. Intentional misspelling or poor use of grammar
   B. Used with special expression such as *signed, labeled,* or *marked*
   C. Technical or slang terms

   D. Refer to the word itself
      (Underline or italics is preferred, but quotation marks are also used.)

WORD

   A. I know you don't "wanna."
   B. The letter was signed "Martin Cuzos."

   C. The "rotary sleeve" clutch was used on the new model. No matter how we ask Bill, he "ain't workin' with ya."
   D. Delete "often" in the second sentence.

3. Use quotation marks to show the DIRECT WORDS of a speaker.
   A. Within a sentence

   B. Within another quotation
   C. Long quotations
      • Within text

      • Blocked off (acceptable but not preferred)

DIRECT WORDS

   A. Bill said, "I want to finish the report."
      "This meeting will now come to order," the director announced.
      "Marie," her friend said, "you must finish this project."
   B. Tom said, "Joe's comment was simply, 'Ugh.' "
   C.
      • The speaker closed with these remarks: "The future of this organization is in your hands. We can grow and prosper or languish. The choice is yours." The speaker received a standing ovation.
      • Phyllis showed her feelings when she replied this way:

         "We will not care about the new report until it is complete. Yet you may express my concern to all of the other staff members. No excuses will be allowed."

Usage Notes:
• Place periods and commas inside the quotation marks.
• Place semicolons and colons outside the quotation marks.
• Place dashes and question marks inside or outside the quotation marks depending on whether the sense applies to all or part.
• Long quotations indented from both right and left margins receive no quotation marks.

COMPACT HYPHEN SUMMARY

1. Use hyphens in COMBINED word forms.
   A. Compound nouns

   B. Compound adjectives

   C. Combined phrases

COMBINED

A. make-believe
   money-maker
   close-up
B. high-pressure hose
   government-owned equipment
   short-term loan
   10-yard gain
C. Hole-in-the-wall gang
   stick-in-the-mud
   never-say-die
   mother-in-law

---

2. Use hyphens in INTERNAL word forms.
   A. Some prefixes

   B. Word separations (end of a line)

   (Note: Consult a current dictionary when using hyphens with prefixes or for word divisions.)

INTERNAL

A. (misreading)   re-create
   (capital letter)   anti-British
   (*ex-* and *self-*) ex-president
   (double vowel)   semi-independent
B. The legislature will not appropriate the funds.

---

3. Use hyphens for MECHANICS.
   A. Numbers

   B. Unusual or extended pronunciations

   C. Letters as letters

   D. Suspended forms

MECHANICS

A. twenty-three
   two-fifths
   A 4-2 victory really pleased the coach.
   pages 234-238
B. G-g-glad you could make it.
   Say a-a-h.
C. The spelling champ spelled *receive* r-e-c-e-i-v-e to win the round.
D. She taught a group of six- and seven-year-olds.
   Lumber may be purchased in 8-, 12-, and 16-foot lengths.

COMPACT APOSTROPHE SUMMARY

1. Use apostrophes to indicate POSSESSION.
   A. Singular words
   B. Plural words

POSSESSION

"Plus" Diagram

	Singular	Plural
Regular	boy	boys
Possessive	boy's	boys'

2. Use apostrophes to indicate DELETION (contraction forms).
   A. Numbers
   B. Letters

   C. In dialogue to show pronunciation
   D. Certain invented expressions

DELETION

A. '76   (1976)
B. can't   (cannot)
   doesn't (does not)
   nat'l   (national)
C. "Well, if you are goin', then I am too."
D. The supervisor ok'd the order.

3. Use apostrophes to indicate PLURALS of symbols and abbreviations.
   A. Characters (letters, numbers, or symbols)

   B. Words referred to as words
   C. Abbreviations
      (without is also accepted when abbreviation is all capital letters)

PLURALS

A. a's   3's
   t's   &'s   i's
   I am looking for your size 5's.
B. In your speech you used too many *and's*.
C. CPU's   (CPUs)
   MPI's   (MPIs)

COMPACT APOSTROPHE SUMMARY

1. Use apostrophes to indicate POSSESSION.
   A. Singular words
   B. Plural words

POSSESSION

"Plus" Diagram

	Singular	**Plural**
Regular	boy	boys
Possessive	boy's	boys'

2. Use apostrophes to indicate DELETION (contraction forms).
   A. Numbers
   B. Letters

   C. In dialogue to show pronunciation
   D. Certain invented expressions

DELETION

A. '76   (1976)
B. can't   (cannot)
   doesn't (does not)
   nat'l   (national)
C. "Well, if you are goin', then I am too."
D. The supervisor ok'd the order.

3. Use apostrophes to indicate PLURALS of symbols and abbreviations.
   A. Characters (letters, numbers, or symbols)

   B. Words referred to as words
   C. Abbreviations
   (without is also accepted when abbreviation is all capital letters)

PLURALS

A. a's   3's
   t's   &s   i's
   I am looking for your size 5's.
B. In your speech you used too many *and's.*
C. CPU's (CPUs)
   MPI's (MPIs)

COMPACT END MARKS SUMMARY

1. Use PERIODS to mark the end of a sentence or unit of thought.
   A. Statements
   B. Commands
   C. Itemized lists
      • Numbered items

      • Lettered items

   D. Decimals
   E. Run-in headings

   F. Abbreviations

PERIODS

A. He graduated in 1989.
B. Close the door.
C.
   • These will be the key items you need:
      1. Canteen
      2. Flashlight
      3. Sleeping bag
   • We will need the following:
      a. Garden tools
      b. Seeds
      c. Willingness to work
D. The new budget is 9.4 percent higher.
E. Legislative influences. After the election, several factors influenced the legislative agenda. Most programs were reevaluated. The limited resources would now have to be distributed among several deserving causes.
F. The retailer will meet the requirements of the C.D.I. The corner of Fourth St. and Elm Ave. is one of the busiest in town. Mr. and Mrs. Santiago will attend the reunion.

---

2. Use QUESTION MARKS to end a question or show doubt about a fact.
   A. Direct question
   B. Editorial meaning
      (only as a last resort for clarification)

QUESTION MARKS

A. Will that be all you need?
B. We cannot located the additional 321 (?) registration forms.

---

3. Use EXCLAMATION MARKS to end a sentence or interjection with strong feeling.
   A. Sentence
   B. Interjection

EXCLAMATION MARKS

A. That concert was amazing!
B. Wow! No wonder everyone is talking about the new cars; they are really different.

COMPACT END MARKS SUMMARY

1. Use PERIODS to mark the end of a sentence or unit of thought.
   - A. Statements
   - B. Commands
   - C. Itemized lists
     - Numbered items
     - Lettered items
   - D. Decimals
   - E. Run-in headings
   - F. Abbreviations

PERIODS

- A. He graduated in 1989.
- B. Close the door.
- C.
  - These will be the key items you need:
    1. Canteen
    2. Flashlight
    3. Sleeping bag
  - We will need the following:
    a. Garden tools
    b. Seeds
    c. Willingness to work
- D. The new budget is 9.4 percent higher.
- E. <u>Legislative influences</u>. After the election, several factors influenced the legislative agenda. Most programs were reevaluated. The limited resources would now have to be distributed among several deserving causes.
- F. The retailer will meet the requirements of the C.D.I. The corner of Fourth St. and Elm Ave. is one of the busiest in town.
  Mr. and Mrs. Santiago will attend the reunion.

---

2. Use QUESTION MARKS to end a question or show doubt about a fact.
   - A. Direct question
   - B. Editorial meaning
     (only as a last resort for clarification)

QUESTION MARKS

- A. Will that be all you need?
- B. We cannot located the additional 321 (?) registration forms.

---

3. Use EXCLAMATION MARKS to end a sentence or interjection with strong feeling.
   - A. Sentence
   - B. Interjection

EXCLAMATION MARKS

- A. That concert was amazing!
- B. Wow! No wonder everyone is talking about the new cars; they are really different.